Copyright © 2012 by WIN F
as permitted under the Unite
this publication may be reproduced or distributed in any form or by any
means, or stored in a data base or retrieval system, without the prior
written permission of the publisher.

MW01170237

FIRST EDITION

This publication is designed to provide accurate and authoritative
information n regard to the subject matter covered. It is sold with the
understanding that neither the author nor the publisher is engaged
in rendering legal, accounting, or other professional service. If legal
advice or other expert assistance is required, the services of a competent
professional person should be sought.

> -   From a Declaration of Principles
>   jointly adopted by a Committee of
>   the American Bar Association and a
>   Committee of Publishers.

WIN Publishing books are available at quantity discounts to use
as premiums and sales promotions, or for use in corporate training
programs. For More information, please email jwilhoit@win–rei.com .

ISBN: 978–0–9850027–0–1

About the Author

John Wilhoit is President of Wilhoit Investment Network, LLC (WIN LLC) His career has focused on large–scale multifamily communities including market rate and mixed–finance developments. He has held positions with HUD, AIMCO and the Maryland Housing fund. Mr. Wilhoit's formal education includes a degree in Business from Pepperdine University and a Masters in Urban & Regional Planning from Alabama A&M University.

WIN LLC provides consulting, asset management and market analysis services for multifamily property owners.

Address: WIN LLC
              3610 Buttonwood Drive #200
              Columbia, MO 65201

Telephone: 573–886–8992

Email: jwilhoit@win–rei.com

On the web: www.MultifamilyInsight.com
              www.MultifamilyBooks.com

On LinkedIN: http://www.linkedin.com/in/johnwilhoit

On Twitter: http://www.twitter.com/johnwilhoitjr

ACKNOWLEDGEMENTS

Thanks to my many mentors that have broadened my horizons both professionally and personally. To name a few, they are; Mrs. Alice Allen, John S. Wilhoit, Sr., Mr. George Eaton, Mr. Richard Mendenhall and Mr. John Brown.

As I have ventured into internet and print media, my greatest advocates have been Mr. Ernest Oriente of PowerHour and Mr. Kerry Kirby of Multifamily Biz.

Ernest F. Oriente, a business coach since 1995 [28,500 hours], a property management industry professional since 1988— the author of SmartMatch Alliances...the founder of PowerHour, and PowerHour SEO has a passion for coaching his clients on executive leadership, hiring and motivating property management SuperStars, traditional and Internet SEO/SEM marketing, competitive sales strategies, and high leverage alliances for property management teams.

To subscribe to Ernest free property management newsletter go to: www.powerhour.com . PowerHour® is based in Olympic–town... Park City, Utah, at 435.615.8486, by E–mail or visit their website: Ernest also runs the #1 LinkedIn group in the world for property management success.

Kerry Kirby is founder of *MultifamilyBiz.com* is owned and operated *365 Connect,* a New Orleans, Louisiana based technology solutions provider to the multifamily industry. *365 Connect* has created an array of technology platforms that work in unison with each other to market, lease and retain residents in multifamily communities. Today, *365 Connect* is the leader in designing and delivering award–winning web–based multifamily technology platforms with an array of products ranging from online leasing centers and interactive resident platforms to *MultifamilyBiz.com*, a powerful and robust B2B industry portal.
MultifamilyBiz.com has grown to become one of the largest sites

in the industry for news, press releases, webcasts and a host of resources. From the latest industry news, member posted press releases, to its robust vendor directories, *MultifamilyBiz.com* is dedicated to providing a suite of focused, leading–edge, online tools and resources designed to maximize and accelerate commercial activities in the multifamily marketplace. For more information regarding *MultifamilyBiz.com* and its services visit: www.MultifamilyBiz.com

To my wife…

Dr. Della Streaty–Wilhoit

Table of Contents

Demographics and Market Analysis – Chapter 3

Financing – Chapter 4

Opinion – Chapter 5

INTRODUCTION

The objective of this writing is to have a compilation of knowledge on multifamily acquisitions and property management in one place at one time as a learning and reference guide for real world education and explanation of how to acquire and management commercial multifamily assets.

This book is a collection of the most popular articles as presented on Multifamily Insight's blog. These articles focus on multifamily acquisitions, property management, market analysis and real estate finance. The fifth category is Opinion with the focus being multifamily and the American economy.

We attempt to present here "ever–green" vignettes that will serve the reader for many years into the future. Like Adam Smith's Invisible Hand, many of the principles within have a long history of being true. More specifically, I hope the thoughts presented will serve as a touchstone to expand your knowledge in the profession of multifamily acquisitions and property management.

Thank you for purchasing this work. It is the culmination of writing over a two year span. The writing is not the hard part; it is the sitting to write that was most difficult.

Chapter 1

Multifamily Acquisitions

Five Biggest Mistakes Multifamily Buyers Make

There are 1,001 potential mistakes in any purchase of multifamily assets that await the non–professional. My objective here is to highlight only a few, some obvious, some not so obvious. For this writing, I am referring to multifamily properties purchased in the prices range of $2–$10 million dollars. This represents a slice of multifamily investments where many people start; those with an interest in the asset class, but not necessarily full–time professionals devoting their daylight hours to running a multifamily business. Following are at the top of my list of common crash points

Crash point: when the issue at hand is greater than your ability to fix it with cash or practical experience.

1. **Inexperience**. Newby's (Newby: someone who has read "books" and books only. i.e., an individual with no practical experience) ALWAYS under–estimate the level of labor required to run the business. While multifamily management is not rocket science there are multiple skill sets required for success. As with McDonald's, whereas anyone can make a hamburger, there's only one company making them by the billion. Why? Systems. They have systems in place that are reliable, transferable and highly structured. And their labor force is trained accordingly. Just this week I heard from a good property manager sharing the job she was applying for went to the "girl friend" of the owner. This is no way to run a multi–million dollar business.

2. **Lack of Dedication**. The multifamily business is not a "hobby" or part–time business. In fact, multifamily management can be a 24 hour business. No different from exercise (and I'm the last one to talk about exercise) seeing measurable results requires not only time, but dedication and effort.

3. **Under Capitalization**. Having <u>little or no cash on the balance sheet</u> is a recipe for disaster. This topic should be a blog unto itself, a book, an encyclopedia of explanation. Business School's teach ratios about cash as a percentage of sales. Consider not less than one month's revenue for cash reserves. While income can be static expenditures can vary widely.

4. **No Capital Expenditure Planning.** Capex is and will always be. <u>Capital expenditures (CAPEX or capex) are expenditures creating future benefits</u>. A capital expenditure is incurred when a business spends money either to buy fixed assets or to add to the value of an existing fixed asset with a useful life that extends beyond the taxable year (<u>http://en.wikipedia.org/wiki/Capital_expenditures</u>). This expense category must be planned and accounted for in annual budgets. Multifamily real estate is a fixed asset class with long operational demands and high capital requirements. Planning for Cap Ex means known "surprises" are not a surprise.

5. **Buying too small– no economies of scale**. There's just no meaningful method for running a 54 unit deal as efficient as running a 154 unit deal. The expenditures in every category are going to be higher (on a per unit basis) with a small property. Now, this is no reason to stay away from the boutiques (<u>boutique: quality multifamily properties under 100 units</u>). This is just a note to remind all to measure apples with apples at time of acquisition.

Construction Starts Lag and Why this is News

If you have only been in the multifamily housing business from 2005 to 2010 you've lived through three cycles; credit elasticity that exceeded the realm of sustainability, a period with vacancy practically doubling in short order, and recovery (assumed recovery). Granted, like with politics, all property is local and competes on a local basis. National trends act as guides to future activity at the local level.

As a multifamily property owner, here are a few things <u>you cannot control</u>; weather, economic meltdowns, historic unemployment and credit availability. Layer a few of these in a single market and surviving selling ice to the Eskimo's seems like an easier task. However (weren't you just hoping for a however?) as an intelligent investor in multifamily, there are a few things <u>you can control;</u> where you acquire assets. This is often determined by your view of past, current and future multifamily housing construction starts.

Its one thing to identify current housing needs in a specific market, quite another to determine future needs (meaning competition). Both are necessary to aggregate an opinion on identifying acquisition candidates and hold times.

In late August 2005 Hurricane Katrina hits News Orleans. This is a historic event. There is loss of life and property. And migration. For a short season the population of Baton Rouge roughly doubled from 225,000 to over 500,000 people. Today, the city is approximately 275,000 people. Anyone who built an apartment development in Baton Rouge in 2004 (that was still standing after the hurricane) looked like a genius. What does this have to do with construction starts?

To wit: Posted April 12, 2010 from www.builderonline. com: Steady Growth in Residential Construction, Upkeep Spending Forecast Thru '14 "...spending on multifamily buildings will drop 12% this year and 8% in 2011 before turning around in 2012 and rising 28% that year, 8% in 2013 and 9% in 2014. In constant dollar terms, the annual expenditures will go from $31.34 billion in 2010 to $43.31 billion in 2014. "Multifamily construction has been impacted severely by tight credit and will not recover until credit loosens".

Some trends are just plain obvious and looking at projected population growth in an area AND housing starts (and multifamily starts) will provide an investor with ground level intelligence as to future occupancy and rent growth potential. Job growth, the type of jobs being created and the clustering of employment centers within proximity to multifamily all impact vacancy and rent growth.

Market specific multifamily housing starts, and their impact on rent growth is directly correlated to changes in population growth, income growth and job creation.

Making a determination about population growth and aligning this information with the number of housing and multifamily housing starts will provide guidance on future vacancy and rent growth. These two factors have significant impact on multifamily property value. This is why it's important to keep an eye on multifamily housing starts.

The Deal Driver Missing Today

Today's reality is that cash is king. So how does one buy apartment complexes with no cash?   Many do this through the use of a cash alternative. For multifamily properties to trade 1031 Tax Free Exchanges are a significant provider of equity (cash) driving transactions.

Depending on the market, 1031 Exchanges can represent two–thirds (2/3) of all transactions driving multifamily acquisitions activity. With limited 1031 Exchange activity occurring there are fewer sales/trades in multifamily.   This is a simple fact.

The IRS defines a 1031 Exchange as follows: To qualify for Section 1031 of the Internal Revenue Code, the properties exchanged must be held for productive use in a trade or business.

Stocks, bonds, and other properties are listed as expressly excluded by **Section 1031 of the** Internal Revenue Code, though securitized properties are not excluded. The properties exchanged must be "like–kind", *i.e.*, of the same nature or character, even if they differ in grade or quality. Personal properties of a like class are like–kind properties. Personal property used predominantly in the United States and personal property used predominantly elsewhere are not like–kind properties. *(http://en.wikipedia.org/wiki/Internal_ Revenue_Code_section_1031)*

 In 2007 Sam Zell sold Equity Office to Blackrock for over $38 billion dollars.   The U.S. recession began soon after. The size and scope of this deal was so large, I believe the entire real estate industry held their breath for a full three minutes at the conclusion of the sale.

And what happens after a large room full of people tries to hold their breath for three minutes? There will be a whole lot of gasping going on. This was the height of the market for residential property also. Homes in southern California have fallen in value some 40% since. More in Nevada and Arizona.   But before the fall there was greed.

Greed: excessive desire to acquire or possess more (especially more material wealth) than one needs or deserves, avarice: reprehensible acquisitiveness; insatiable desire for wealth (personified as one of the deadly sins) wordnetweb.princeton.edu/perl/webwn.

Mr. Zell was not greedy. Mr. Zell was made a bona–fide offer and concluded it was reasonable. He accepted and sold. However, those following in his wake (all too often) thought of themselves as mini–Zell's, whereas; if Sam can get $300 a square foot certainly I can also. Not true. And as sellers attempted to ratchet prices yet "one more time" buyer's balked (slowing their step– not wanting to be the last one standing without a chair when the music stopped).

Lenders also took notice as their default rates were beginning to rise based on valuations not supported by "current" operating numbers. As credit tightened prices (and 1031's) began a gradual decline. The death spiral increased its velocity as Lehman collapsed in the fall of 2008.

In your local market, for deal sizes that fit your profile identify the number of properties that are changing hands via 1031. This is another barometer for tracking the level of sales activity (and the number of players) with whom you must compete for deals. Fewer 1031's means fewer direct competitors for multifamily properties in your marketplace. Good to know before being in the throes of negotiations.

Know Your Exit Strategy before Buying

For this post, we are "backing into" how to buy multifamily properties by starting with the question; how do you decide when to sell a multifamily asset?

Sell, sell, sell! That's my favorite Jim Cramer button. The Mad Money talk show host has a myriad of sound effects at his disposal but for some odd reason that's the only one I seem to hear. It always catches my attention.

How many things do you buy with the intent to sell– even before you buy?

Every multifamily property we own is for sale. Now, there is not a "for sale" sign on the curb with blinking lights. But it is for sale. Every asset class has an end game strategy to sell. Excluding short–sellers, the objective is to sell the asset for more than you paid for it. The question is when and for how much? Tie this in with a present value analysis (time value of money) and we can estimate our return on investment. Of course, some of us are better estimators than others. Some are lucky (I don't believe in luck but I do believe the best prepared seem to be luckier than those that are not prepared). My objective here is to ask you to "pause and ponder". The market doesn't care whether or not you need to sell. But the cyclical nature of the multifamily market does provide certain opportunities to sell. Are you listening for these signals?

If every property you own could be sold for twice what you paid for it the question is; is it for sale?

Next question: if a cold call came to your phone asking for a selling price of your apartments do you know that number? If not, how long would it take you to get back to a potential buyer? The point is that in the open marketplace there are always some buyers that <u>need</u> to buy. If one happens to walk into your door are you prepared?

So why is this blog on selling multifamily assets under the heading of acquisitions?   Because I want you to think about a sale of the asset acquired – even before you buy it. What market attributes will attract the next buyer?

How much rent growth do you need to meet IRR targets **internal rate of return:** http://en.wikipedia.org/wiki/Internal_rate_of_return. The internal rate of return on an investment or potential investment is the *annualized effective compounded return rate* that can be earned on the invested capital.   Can addressing deferred maintenance bring the asset back to market at a higher value? How soon and at what costs?

 Our company acquires apartment assets for long–term hold. We seldom buy anything that we would not want to own ten years into the future. With that said, we track the value of assets under management well and know our markets.   Whereas we are not actively seeking to sell we know the current market value of our assets. Therefore, if an unsolicited offer comes in the door we are in a position to respond. And quickly.   When opportunity knocks, it seldom knocks loudly.   Nor does it stick around forever while you decide whether or not to open the door.

The better you know the intrinsic value of your multifamily assets the better prepared you are to make them work for you. Sometimes that means selling and re–deploying proceeds even if taxable (not often, mind you, but it could happen).

Success requires preparation
There are no shortcuts.   How do you prepare?   Know your markets. Read. Be yourself. Read great books. Network. Find like–minded people. Remove pride. Don't fake it. Be willing to say " I don't know".   Believe in yourself and your skill set.

What NOT to Buy

A Capital Needs Assessment (CNA) can assist multifamily buyers in quantifying deferred maintenance and creating a timeline for disbursement of funds to remedy immediate repairs and longer term capital outlays. In many instances, it can tell you what <u>not</u> to buy.

Few people are doing business as usual. In multifamily, this means capital expenditures get deferred and routine maintenance is extended (meaning put off unit later).   With smaller deals (those under $5M) you can sometimes get away with calling on local trade professionals to assess roofing, HVAC, electrical and plumbing.   As the deal size increases the necessity of a accomplishing a professionally prepared CNA grows more critical.

Once completed, your Capital Needs Assessment is a negotiating tool, one that can create savings and profit.   It can also solidify underlying value. It's good to know if a targeted investment property acquisition will need, for example, $250,000 in total repairs, better to know that half this number is immediate with the balance invested over a five or ten year term.

The Capital Needs Assessment (CNA) prepares a long–term budget strategy to ensure long–term viability of a development

Buying an apartment building is not an impulse purchase.   The multifamily acquisition process is a significant time commitment but one that can be very rewarding.   Including a CNA into the acquisition process allows a buyer greater confidence. Beyond simple maintenance, any investment of several million dollars (or higher) should have as part of the buyers due diligence an assessment of capital needs.

 Warren Buffet purchased BNSF Railway this year. Soon after the closing on the $26 Billion Dollar deal Mr. Buffet called the CEO and said "I'm looking forward to our first century together". Indeed, Mr. Buffet knows how to plan for the future.

Think of a CNA as a property "snapshot" that captures the functional health on a specific date, similar to how an appraisal captures the estimated value of a property on a certain date. It may be the least expensive insurance you ever buy. Consider that sellers (some sub–human) continue to obtain insurance checks for wind and/or hail damage and pocket the funds versus doing the repairs… being more than willing to sell you this same property with known damage in place and not disclosed.

The recession has made everyone "cut back" on upkeep that historically was part of standard operating procedure. Scheduled maintenance becomes *deferred* maintenance after a certain period of time. Routine maintenance such as changing air filters and regular pest control become "optional" to some owners when cash flow gets tight.

As a buyer of investment property, while there may be more assets to choose from, consider that sellers are not predisposed to share maintenance schedules. While this is not fraudulent consider a lack of records to be, at the very least, suspect.

Excluding developments that were built to fail (with poor quality workmanship or materials) many can maintain functionality for fifty to one hundred years if well maintained. This type of longevity seldom occurs accidentally. It requires planning, investment and proactive stewardship.

Similar to noting that a rent roll is not the whole story on the revenue side, so too does a CNA point to deficiencies below the surface. I'm not referring exclusively to structural failing, but seal & seam, fit & finish that will require investment dollars well beyond normalized routine maintenance. The $500 million dollar asking price doesn't put you off the CNA would be a startling eye–opener.

A perfect example of a functionally failing development is the Watergate in Washington DC. It's been for sale for years– at least most of it has been for sale. Not only are there multiple small owners, but a hotel, commercial office and retail space, varying lease holds and a helipad. Where do you start? It's got location. It's got name recognition. It's got big problems. Assuming

 In today's marketplace there are seldom multiple offers, therefore, as a serious buyer, now is an opportune time to negotiate for "days". The first "days" to negotiate for is an extended time to perform due diligence. With this extended time you can accomplish a thorough review without having earnest money at risk.

No Money Down is Not Dead (Part I)

I promise.

I promise that for as long as this blog has my stamp on it to never, ever, under any circumstances to promote multifamily "no money down" deals. Except for today.

While I say "no money down is not dead", it is on life support. I submit that most "no cash in" multifamily deals should not have been done in the first place, primarily for reasons of inexperience on the buyer's part. That said there are a few instances where no cash deals have their place.

Multifamily "no money down" deals are hard work. Really hard work. Once purchased, based on the high level of leverage they are even harder work.

So why would anyone want to do a nothing down deal?

There are two extremes where zero down can work:

1. **To get in the game.** Many people are interested in knowing how to buy apartment complexes with no cash. It's a big draw for a novice to buy an asset with no cash. Some people want in the game so bad they will agree to any terms for the sake of controlling the deal. NO! As the saying goes, pride often goes before a fall. Getting in the game is a worthy pursuit, but don't shoot yourself in the foot as you leave the starting blocks with your first deal.

As I have said in other post– know your exit strategy before buying. Consider also; what makes you so special that this deal is being offered to you? What's the upside potential if rents remain flat for an extended period? What is the Debt Service Coverage (DSC) on closing day? Is this sustainable?

Individuals wanting to acquire and manage multifamily assets need to know there are multiple pieces to making a high leverage deal work. Buying a one or two million dollar deal with high leverage not only requires skill on the acquisitions piece, but also in operations.

Being able to buy the deal is not the same as being able to manage the deal. And whereas management expertise can be picked up along the way on a cute little duplex, the same cannot be said for a 100 unit multifamily deal. No one opens a restaurant and then starts searching for a cook. Management is still a key aspect– even more so with tight margins based on high leverage.

As a straight passive investor in a high leverage deal there is even more risk. Perhaps you've put up your balance sheet for a piece of ownership. Unless you are going into the deal with a very experienced operator– run! Experienced operator often excludes most family members, those you've only met online and third cousins, twice removed. And anyone that you would not trust with the actual cash (this is the real crux of the matter). If you wouldn't invest cash in the deal, you probably shouldn't be putting up your balance sheet as a passive investor.

While so much of this post may seem discouraging, the point is really to be prepared and know the risk. Have a plan of action from day one. Have a backup plan and an exit strategy…. All prior to closing.

In Part II we will discuss why experienced owners may consider adding a "nothing down deal" to their existing portfolio.

No Money Down is Not Dead (Part II)

In Part 1, we discussed the inexperienced multifamily buyer and reasons for their willingness to enter into a nothing down deal. In this post, we turn to the experienced operator/owner and discuss their motivations for pursuing a high–leverage multifamily acquisition candidate. In Part I, the motivation suggested for the new investor is to **Get in the Game**. For experienced investors....

2. **You are already in the game**; you know the game well and adding an additional multifamily asset, albeit highly leveraged, doesn't negatively impact your balance sheet or cash flow. It can be particularly rewarding to acquire an additional asset in a city where you have existing operations.

New and expanded economies of scale including the new acquisition may actually lower your overall costs of operations (on a per unit basis) as management and maintenance personnel are spread over additional units. This is where an "OK" asset can become a driver to increasing portfolio–wide Net Operating Income (NOI). The use of over–leverage, of course, is a two–edge sword.

It's just not funny how short–term financing is technically really short–term. Really. People wait in line for hours to ride a two–minute roller coaster. That's what short–term financing is like. We put in the hours and suffer the wait to obtain the debt, and the ride is over in two minutes (OK– it could be a two–year loan but you get the point– it's still short–term).

The best protection against having a quality deal implode is to secure long–term financing on as much of the debt as possible. From that point, your financing focus can be on replacing any remaining debt with equity. The ancillary debt can be addressed through the sale of fractional interest in the property, from the sale of other assets and/or from cash flow from the purchased asset or other assets.

Cash flow from other apartment assets in the portfolio can be utilized to sustain the newly purchased, highly levered asset (if necessary). But this should be transitional, not a way of life. Cash reserves, cash flow, and impound accounts build a safety net for an owner adding a high–leverage deal into the fold.

 In conclusion, while nothing down is not dead, it is a risky business. It's not for the faint of heart or those that cry easily or lose sleep about rent collections. If nothing down deals were an asset class I would estimate that less than two percent of all multifamily deals fall into this category. So while they do come along, (when they do) its best to be prepared with abilities to manage not only the property but the increased risk associated with high leverage.

Buying in Your Own Zip Code

Information about how to buy multifamily properties is on every corner through seminars, books and late night television. But where should one buy apartments? What location? How does an investor select apartment market areas for acquisitions? Too often market selection is based on criteria completely unrelated to sound long–term multifamily ownership strategy.

As a commercial investor in multifamily property I believe it is difficult to justify buying a multifamily asset based on the decision my wife and I made as to where to raise the kids. To me, that's like having to buy a car in Detroit or Brazil because that's where they make them. What does that have to do with the value of the underlying asset?

There is not necessarily a correlation between quality apartments developments and your very own zip code

Frankly, in many instances, I believe investors are better served with some distances (measured in miles, not blocks) to avoid the temptation of micro–management.

I'm guessing perhaps five of the last ten things you have purchased were made in China. Been to China lately? Me neither. Quality multifamily properties were NOT built based on your home base decision point. Therefore, I submit, your decision as to where to acquire apartments should ALSO not be based on this same data point.

Justifying a flight to safety by staying close to home negates most requisites to good underwriting

Insurance companies do not sell insurance only to those within a stone's throw of the home office. Neither should you acquire multifamily assets based on where your family resides. Granted, it could happen. Let your underwriting standards select locations starting with proximity to jobs and job centers. Not parks. Not drive time to your favorite pub or ice cream parlor.

Spock, my cape! We go forth toward the great frontier! As long as it's in our zip code

Flight to Safety and Close to Home Have No Correlation. When it comes to preservation of capital close to home does not necessarily correlate with higher levels of safety or yield.   Recognizing that many people like to "kick the tires" of their investments, it seems that real estate is one of the few investments where proximity to one's personal residence is a factor.

Does Warren Buffet Buy only in Omaha?

For those with stock and bond investments, if you own AT&T, is it important to you to know the whereabouts of every AT&T facility or each and every infrastructure project that GE is building? Why then, do investors believe that if they can drive by their multifamily assets that the property is perhaps better secured? I just don't see the correlation.   Quality multifamily assets are quality assets. If the investor is a resident of San Francisco and their investment is in Austin, Texas what's the beef?

Follow quality and yield, not proximity to your own house

There is ALWAYS a correlation between the quality of multifamily assets and the income derived.   We can spare over degrees of freedom, age factors, location of course, amenities etc.   When seeking safety of principal what do you buy? Quality. Quality over quantity. Quality over warm and fuzzy feelings. Quality over price. Quality over mature landscaping. Quality over proximity to your own house. Did I mention quality?

"Buy land, they're not making it anymore" – Mark Twain

I grew up in southern California. I've lived on the east coast and now in the Midwest. When my wife and I first arrived in the Midwest (after flying over one thousand miles of open land) we sat down with a Realtor in a city of less than 100,000 people with the nearest big city being over one hundred miles away.

We shared with the Realtor that we wanted a home with one or two acres and certain other particulars. Before we could finish she pursed her lips and shook her head telling us that such a property was not to be found…. they just didn't build homes on one and two acre parcels around these parts. What? We found another agent.

And so it goes. Apparently, whatever apartments we are looking for are not to be found. Oh, you want that in blue? We only have gray today. You want a low–rise apartment building in Chicago. Sorry, but we've got some great garden units across the lake…

My point is once you have decided on geography and sub–market specifications– do not deviate from the level of quality selected. I will suggest, based on experience that attempting to stay in a single market and acquire multifamily assets of quality is a difficult proposition.

Be willing to expand the search area outside of your own zip code, careful to stay with quality multifamily assets as defined by you. Long–term investors in the multifamily asset class buy quality based on factors not related to their own residence. I submit this is a good practice.

Why Grow Your Portfolio?

Multifamily assets have a place in a well diversified investment portfolio. In 2010 we continue to survive the "great recession".   Last spring, the Dow dropped nine percentage points in one day only to bounce back up the next day. High unemployment persists. Yet people will always need a place to call home.

Food and Shelter– kind of important
Why should you want to grow your multifamily portfolio? Because it will help to feed your family in more ways than one.

I worked in Virginia sometime ago. There was a little breakfast/lunch restaurant in the basement of our office building that was good for a quick meal. The owner was always happy to see her customers.

I asked her once how she seemed to always be happy even though working in a basement every day with no sunshine. Her response was; "I am very happy to feed my customers because they help me to feed my family, and that makes me very happy".

Diversification, Scale, Liquidity and Yield   So how can owning apartments help to feed your family? Partly by offering **diversification**, **scale, liquidity** and **yield,** all playing their part to enhance the whole of the investment.

One can be diversified by asset type (stocks, bonds, real estate, etc) and also by geography (by region, country or hemisphere). Multifamily is an important asset class that offers diversification by geography and quality.

Having scale in apartments means spreading fixed costs over additional units with limited impact on marginal costs. Example: adding 100 units to a portfolio of 400 units in the same city will not increase management costs by 25% in a centralized management system.

Of the major asset classes within real estate (office, industrial, retail and multifamily) I would argue that multifamily is the most liquid. This is one of the most compelling reasons to invest in this asset class. Add geographic diversity and risk is further diluted.

Yield is a function of risk. Risk is best controlled by direct management control. The better the management, the more impact management will have on yield. Spending money on management is not just an investment/expense. It is an investment/investment in quality control and risk management.

Portfolio Size Matters

In multifamily ownership, economies of scale play an important role in controlling costs and in creating expansion opportunities. Banking relationships, professional service providers and others will sometimes determine pricing and service levels based on the volume of business they are generating from your umbrella of holdings.

Portfolio allocation theory suggests that an investment portfolio should have between 5% and 15% of assets in real estate (excluding your personal residence). Thus, investors should have between $50,000 and $150,000 in real estate for every one million dollars in net worth.

Investment Real Estate Provides Yield

Behold the yield generators! They are:

- Income – as derived from rents or other ancillary income generated
- Tax shelter – provided by depreciation of the physical asset over time
- Appreciation – from increasing rental revenue over time
- Mortgage pay down – using rental income to decrease mortgage debt

Multifamily is not the only alternative investment to stocks and bonds but it is a sound, solid asset class with legs and less volatility than commodities, oil and gas or pork bellies.

Multifamily assets may not be all that exciting or sexy (any more than that basement restaurant). But apartment ownership, when applied with skill, will be there to feed your family as your investment provides a roof for others to live under.

5 Ways Investors Make Money

People know there is money to be made in multifamily real estate. But how, exactly, does an investor derive yield from owning apartments? Yes, there is income from rents. But what else– how do we get from a review of the income statement to determining investor yield? There are five ways to make money with multifamily assets:

- Appreciation – increase in value over time
- Income – derived from rents and other income
- Depreciation – tax benefits
- Mortgage reduction – reducing debt through principal payments

An investor can potentially benefit from all four categories as a real estate owner. Whether passive or hands–on, these four categories can provide a component of investor yield What is the fifth?

Quality Asset Management
The fifth method for making money in real estate is professional expertise brought to the deal – <u>asset management</u>. Specifically; management that controls costs and guides or directs capital expenditures.

Controlling Controllable Expenses
The asset management function brings a high level of expertise to increasing direct and indirect income and controlling short and long–term expenditures. Succinctly: controlling controllable expenses. Without this fifth "corner" being applied to real estate ownership the other four contributors to investor yield can erode rapidly.

Here is an exercise you may want to try. Take each component from the list above and attach a dollar amount to each one. Here is an example for a $5,000,000 asset.

- Appreciation – assuming 1.5% appreciation, the increase in value each year is $75,000 annually
- Income – let's assume $25,000 net distributed each year
- Depreciation – tax benefits. This requires some research as every one's tax bracket is different. Let's say, $18,000 in actual tax savings for a given year
- Mortgage reduction – reducing debt through principal payments. On a $3,500,000 mortgage, principal reduction is around $50,000 annually. Total: *$168,000*

Given a cash investment of $1,500,000 the first year yield is 11.2%. In this example, asset management would probably raise this to the low teens. This is an ultra–simplistic example, I know, but it provides you with a guide to determining annual investor yield utilizing all of the components available to the investor.

Why Buy Now?

This post is not about how to buy apartments, but when to buy apartments.

Is 2011 the best time to buy apartments in a generation? While commercial real estate is crashing all around, multifamily pricing has remained relevantly stable. Capitalization rates have had some upward pressure but there's been no great glut of Class A properties washing up on our shores at bargain basement prices. Winter gloves always go on sale at the first sign of spring, right? Apparently this does not apply to apartment buildings.

The best time to buy a straw hat is in the dead of winter

Hindsight is always 20/20. And the good old days are always seen with rose colored glasses. Here are some reasons to consider buying apartments now:

- Pricing constraints (read: no rent growth) has kept sales prices on a per unit basis in a very tight band (market specific)

- Any one positive will begin to increase valuations, such as; lower unemployment, clearing of the foreclosure backlog, the White Sox winning the Pennant

- Construction starts do not turn on a dime. Once multifamily construction picks up there will be several quarters of lag for this new product to impact the marketplace

Stability is the word I use most often when referring to multifamily ownership. Stability in income and predictable cash flows. If looking only at the last two years, that's a hard statement to make with a straight face. Review any recent ten year term, however, and the statement holds true. The multifamily sector as a whole holds its own very well as compared to other investment alternatives and within the real estate sector.

The best time to buy Easter eggs is the day after Easter

So if there is no fire sale occurring in the multifamily sector, in these, the worst of times, what happens when things turn around??? Dare I say prices will rebound? We've had limited rent growth the last two years (an under–statement), very low construction starts and no inflation to prop up prices. Yet pricing has remained remarkably firm.

While a great many people continue to look upward thinking "the best deal ever" is going to drop out of the sky and into their lap, real buyers and real sellers are doing deals. Transactions at fair prices are occurring, often on an all cash basis. My suggestion to buyers is that a historic review will reflect 2011 was a good time to acquire apartments– at fair prices in good markets.

Gartman's Rules of Trading

Mr. Dennis Gartman is the author of the Gartman Letter, a subscription based investment newsletter (http://www. thegartmanletter.com/). One of Mr. Gartman's well known writings is *Gartman's Rules to Trading* representing things he's learned in a long career of investing.

In this post I will attempt to take a few of his rules and apply them to multifamily acquisitions. Buying apartments, as an investment class, has many similarities to other investments in that many people make the same mistakes. To wit, Mr. Gartman's Rule #1:

RULE #1. Never, ever, under any circumstance, should one add to a losing position … not EVER!

Meaning… in multifamily acquisitions no matter how much you may "love" that deal that's losing $150,000 each of the last two years, under no circumstances should you contemplate purchasing a sister property in that same market. As if that will make everything all better. No Gracie, it will not!

Building wealth requires knowing the winners from the losers in your field of play. Doubling up in the same field (read: market or sub–market) will not right the ship on a losing proposition.

RULE # 2. Never, ever, under any circumstance, should one add to a losing position … not EVER!

As you can see, he is very sincere about Rule #1. Mr. Gartman remarks:

"Averaging down into a losing trade is the only thing that will assuredly take you out of the investment business. This is what took LTCM out. This is what took Barings Brothers out; this is what took Sumitomo Copper out, and this is what takes most losing investors out."

RULE #10. To trade/invest successfully, think like a fundamentalist; trade like a technician.

A further quote from Mr. Gartman:

"It is obviously imperative that we understand the economic fundamentals that will drive a market higher or lower, but we must understand the technicals as well. When we do, then and only then can we, or should we, trade".

In real estate parlance; is the property fundamentally sound? Does the greater market and , specifically, the sub–market meet or exceed stated investment criteria?

Has Engineering willfully signed off on the acquisition or were they "coerced" to provide a certain conclusion? (News flash: yes, people sometimes fool themselves and others to meet objectives that are un–related to the actual asset being acquired). Are most of the known warts accounted for in the financial forecast?

In apartment speak consider the "technicals" to mean categories such as financial underwriting, demographic trends and their impact, retail growth in the market and job creation. And within job creation, being able to break down the type of job creation in the market; projected and near term growth in professional versus service sector jobs, as an example.

Rule #13. Do more of that which is working and less of that which is not.

In life, as investors and as property managers… what better mantra!

Internet Millions One Property at a Time

How do you build a solid multifamily portfolio? Usually one property at a time. Sure, there are aggregated portfolios for sale for those that have portfolio acquisition money. But for the rest of us, we buy one property, and then we buy another. And after a while, we have a portfolio.

My first on–line real estate purchase was in 2003. It was a single–family house in a nice neighborhood. I made my second on–line real estate purchase in 2005 paying just over two million dollars ($2.0M) for a multifamily apartment complex. I've been hooked on Internet search ever since.

Shop Globally, Buy Locally
It's an everyday occurrence that people shop the Internet to learn about product features and prices. Then, very often, they will look to purchase that same item locally based on price and availability. The same is true for Internet multifamily property shopping. Most shoppers are looking for a local property. It's a mistake, however, to rely exclusively on local resources to identify available multifamily assets. The internet provides us with the ability to search globally for local assets.

Lenders Near and Far
Pick a lender (any lender) and a review of their apartment loan portfolio will reflect mortgage loans near and wide from the home office. Wells Fargo has loans coast to coast. Same with Bank of America and two dozen other lenders.

When looking for a local property make sure the search includes REO (Real Estate Owned) websites of national lenders. One cannot assume that all local property is controlled by local lenders. This leaves too many assets out of the search.

Fannie Mae and Freddie Mac have billions of dollars in assets for sale. Granted, most of their for–sale assets are mortgages, but not all. Some are bread and butter multifamily apartment assets in major cities.

Get Lost, Get Found
Its fine to "get lost" on the Internet for a time while searching for deals. It's not fine to stay lost. Time is money. Have a plan on how to utilize your time on–line while property shopping. Like going to an auction, you price points and market area should be determined in quiet (off line), not in the heat of the moment (while searching).

There's little reason to spend a day looking at multi–million dollar deals if your price point is much lower. Have a plan. Stick to the plan. Focus on finding deals that will work for you. Take into consideration available financing and current financial underwriting standards.

Local Knowledge, Global Search
The biggest time–waster is fooling ourselves in terms of property shopping for deals that are out of our ability to obtain. Even then, accomplishing a global search for a specific locale (one or two markets) only has value when you have superior knowledge about that market.

If you know nothing about a market, why are you searching there? If that's the case… you're just surfing.

Finding a Gold Plated Property (and SWOT)

Just to end the suspense early– there is no such thing as a perfect apartment building. Measure these four things to distinguish gold from copper: Strengths. Weaknesses. Opportunities. Threats.

A partial definition of a quality multifamily asset is one where ownership and management recognizes short–comings and can remedy or address these to compete effectively in the marketplace.

One standard business school technique teaches scenario analysis as a form of triage that can be applied to crisis management. The first thing a manager does in crisis is assess the following:

Strengths, Weaknesses, Opportunities, Threats (SWOT)

There are textbooks on SWOT analysis. Very often this methodology can be applied to a stabilized multifamily asset with the luxury of time (time to think, time to plan). Re–stating this in multifamily terminology, we can get closer to owning and operating a gold plated multifamily asset by;

Recognizing our strengths and weaknesses while taking advantage of opportunities concurrent with minimizing threats.

Following are every–day occurrences for multifamily professionals engaged in acquisitions and dispositions. In these examples, for simplicity, we are excluding references to mortgage workouts and short–sales.

Scenario #1. The perfect apartment complex! Everyone wants one, no one has one for sale and those few that are available are offered at a four cap.

In multifamily acquisitions there is no such thing as "one size fits all". Perceived quality is exceptionally elastic. One person's quality (lots of cash flow) is not the same as for someone else (no taxable distributions).

Determining the long–term objectives of ownership <u>prior to</u> <u>acquisition</u> provides baseline information for determining targeted assets for acquisition. This is another way of saying; have a plan with input from those most impacted by the intended results.

Scenario #2. Investment committee will acquire all you can deliver… at their selected price points with limited consideration given to anything else. Equity sources require your firm to perform all necessary due diligence so they may cherry pick at will.

Even for in–house dispositions teams this sometimes seems to be the case; they work hard, very hard, to identify the best quality assets only to be shot down by the Executive Committee time and time again. Very often, the disconnect here is a matter of relationships and trust.

Multifamily acquisitions cannot be accomplished by "PowerPoint". Acquisitions proceed based on <u>trust</u> and mutual benefit (I'm referring to within the buy–side entity) and relationships within the company.

An imperfect marketplace

Scenario #3. Reality is….

Reality is there are quality assets available for sale every day.

Reality is, at present, there are boat–loads of cash searching for quality assets. But it is an imperfect marketplace, it is a fractured marketplace.

Reality is 1031 Exchanges, at one time, represented two– thirds (2/3) of all transactions driving multifamily acquisitions activity. With limited 1031 Exchange activity occurring there are fewer sales/trades in multifamily.

There are fewer buyers in the marketplace today than five years ago. Many are well capitalized with the luxury of being selective. Then there is everyone else– where we live in the trenches.

Balancing Reality with the Current Day Marketplace

Multifamily acquisitions are being accomplished. Reviewing deals with the assumption that the equity in the deal is your money brings much clarity to deal–making. It also eliminates head games and crystallizes the tasks at hand.

Would you put your money in the deal given the investors objectives? If not, why not and does this reason increase or decrease the attractiveness of the transaction. Place yourself in the chair of the equity investor.

Know your exit strategy prior to purchase

No small task as people and property change over time. Who knew in 2007 what 2008 would bring? Do the best you can to quantify risk. Have good systems, processes and memorialize same through documentation. Communication is key.

Gold plated property? All is in the eyes of the beholder.

How to Validate Rental Income

 When it comes to magic tricks one rule of thumb is to not fool yourself. The same rule applies when selecting multifamily acquisition candidates. There are no short–cuts.

Completing the acquisition of a quality multifamily asset can be an arduous task. There are numerous moving pieces and many "metrics" to measure starting with determining rental revenue.

By revenue I mean rental income. In other blog post we have discussed other income and incremental income. Determining the value of a multifamily acquisition candidate rest squarely on rental income. This is our focus in this blog post.

There are many different names for rental income. Here are some common names: Income, Gross Rents, Gross Potential Rents, Revenue, and Rental Revenue. For purposes of this blog they mean the same thing. Here are three places to begin the process of getting to that real number.

The Rent Roll

Rent Roll. How do you see clear with the consistent "smoke" of glossy reports, fancy brochures and the deluge of information? Start with the rent roll.

An income/expense statement is a starting point for determining value. Use the rent roll as a guide to determining revenue generation. One of the first things to review is whether rental income from the income statement matches the rent roll. If not, why not.

Certainly, most deviations between the rent roll and profit/loss statement can be accounted for. But when the numbers begin to widen (large monthly differentials between Income statement and rent roll) further explanation is required to address the disparity.

Bottom line is if the two never match, how do you know which document to believe; the income statement or the rent roll?

Further due diligence would include a review of 100% of leases files, random conversations with tenants, supervised calls to tenants, etc. These actions all designed to validate, validate and validate revenue numbers.

The Bank Statements

Bank Statements. Let us say the numbers seem to be a bit... bouncy. They're just not adding up. The fastest way to see clear is review bank statements. Statement deposits should correlate quickly with receipts. If not, why not. If yes, you can move on to a review of expenses (that's another blog).

Sometimes you will hear much murmuring with this request for bank statements. Be reasonable, make it a doable thing, but convey its necessity to tie off your due diligence. When buying a long–term asset– it's your money. This is no time to be shy about acquiring facts and figures.

The Unit Inspections

Unit Inspections. For "real time" validation of current income there's nothing that can replace an inspection of one hundred percent of the units on property. That's right... going inside every last unit on property.

Are the units occupied? Do people really live here? This is often accomplished after validation of numbers, but if it's a property with potential but suspect revenue numbers, best to do this earlier in the decision–making process.

Unit inspections are usually saved until later in the due diligence process. Unit inspections are time consuming, but so is chasing a deal where sellers are having a hard time delivering credible paperwork. This allows you to cut your losses (of time and energy) quickly when necessary.

Most often, a random inspection of X units starts this process (5–15% of units). Keep records so there is no need to duplicate later when the 100% inspection is scheduled.

There is always more to do to increase one's comfort level with the numbers. These are some starting points to get the buyer beyond the pretty pictures and reports that were generated three, maybe even six months prior to the property being placed on the market.

Why People Sell

The reasons people sell their owned multifamily assets are many. Very often the trigger point for listing income property has little to do with the property itself and everything to do with ownership. For one, commercial real estate investing is not a part time business. Sometimes people (owners) just get tired of the grind and decide to devote their time to other money making endeavors.

In the last two years we have had limited price appreciation from inflation or rent growth (market specific). Does that mean we never will? Of course not, however, living through the downturn with no help from the capitalistic positives we are accustom to have some owners crying in their soup.

Another reason multifamily owners are selling is because the national unemployment rate has remained consistently high and this directly impacts occupancy. We sometimes forget that figure means nine out of ten people continue to be employed. This fact brings no joy to multifamily property owners accustom to 95% plus occupancy now struggling to maintain 85% occupancy.

Some sell because of financial or operational burnout. Sometimes selling is spurred by just not wanting to have the responsibility anymore; sometimes it's a financial imperative. Then there's age; age of the owners, age of the income property. Here are four reasons multifamily assets are listed for sale:

- Distressed property
- Distressed ownership
- Both – distressed property and ownership
- Neither– distressed property or ownership

In many instances the reason people sell their income property has nothing to do with the property itself. The passing away of a single owner within a group can be the trigger point for listing a multifamily property for sale. Again, this has nothing to do with the quality or operations of the multifamily asset.

In a distressed market everyone wants to know the reason for selling. Like knowing this information is the Holy Grail. It is not. This information is one factor in the "buyer" decision making process. Note that most of the time the information provided is for purposes of motivating the buyer. Caveat Emptor rules!

Consider the psychological aspects of investing in the stock market. Do investors buy or sell strictly based on the financial standing of a particular stock? No– the nuance of information that surfaces about a stock can sometimes have more impact on value than reported numbers. The same is true for of multifamily assets.

Here is my key point: The reason a multifamily seller is selling has nothing whatsoever to do with why a buyer is buying. This statement excludes any reference to "yes but". There is no replacement for serious due diligence on the part of the buyer. Serious due diligence considers the reason the seller is selling from the perspective of the buyer.

Example: GM Files for Bankruptcy. Does that mean you make a run on the nearest GM dealership? The same applies to sellers of multifamily assets. Just because a seller is distressed doesn't mean they are giving away the store.

More to the point: Does GM's bankruptcy have anything to do with your need for a new vehicle? Being in the market to acquire multifamily income property has nothing to do with the motivations of a given seller.

Question: If you know the reason the seller is selling– so what? There are 123 other people with the same information. This information is a single inflection point within the entire buying process.

Reading the tea leaves of why income property is for sale might be a fun hobby, but there is seldom a single reason for selling. Remember, at some price, you can buy anything. The question is: then what? (Exploring buyer motivation is for a different post).

Granted, there are occasions where speed of action is necessary based on the needs of the seller. More importantly, it should be your own due diligence cadence that drives a buying decision– not the needs or desires of the seller. Remember, after closing they go home... never to call or talk to your team again.

When it comes to determining why a multifamily owner is selling, try to refrain from devoting time to conspiracy theories. In the light of day and with good due diligence a buyer can identify outstanding litigation or overt issues undisclosed by an unscrupulous seller.

Reminder: There are no short cuts to quality due diligence and never a reason to close a deal without title insurance. Most people are pretty straight forward. This doesn't mean they desire to share their deepest thoughts on the matter with you.

There are many reasons people sell. For buyers, the focus should be on the reasoning behind the buying decision.

TLC (Timing. Leverage. Competition.)

Timing. Leverage. Competition. TLC. All three play a significant role in completing multifamily acquisitions. It's similar to the old adage for printing services– quality, speed or price; pick any two. Seldom will a single investment property transaction present positive attributes in all three categories.

Real estate, and multifamily real estate, is a slow moving asset class. When the stars align a sale can be completed in perhaps five to seven working days. The norm is 45–60 days. And like any transaction with multiple moving pieces it ain't over till it's' over.

TIMING. There is no such thing as perfect timing except for in hindsight. Timing multifamily buys is no different than attempting to time the stock market. It can happen, but even the "smartest guys in the room" blush when their great buy hits a yield–popping home run.

Timing has to do with availability of product and financing. It's the big "so what". So what if there are deals for sale by the boatload, yet no mortgage loans? So what if mortgage money is plentiful when available inventory is mostly old and dusty.

LEVERAGE. Availability of debt plays an important role in the ability of most buyers to acquire. As CMBS has died off (with a possible comeback pending) and mortgage underwriting has become tighter than most Cuban cigars, the average buyer is removed to the sidelines in favor of all cash buyers.

There are two types of all cash buyers: smart ones and everybody else. My guess is the 80/20 rule applies here whereas twenty percent of the all cash buyers really understand the multifamily asset class and eighty percent are following the herd.

Like people getting into gold at $1,400 an ounce (this being their first purchase ever) or condos in Brazil to flip. How many of the people buying these products really understand their valuation? Perhaps two of ten. Maybe.

COMPETITION. Defining competition is really market specific. Every buyer in the world, even hungry buyers, will not buy a deal in New York City because it's not in their market. It doesn't matter that current supply is tight; new construction is limited, incomes are rising, unemployment is dropping. The market is of no interest to that wealth management group in Rockville Maryland tasks with buying deals in the Washington DC market.

Contrary to this example, I would bet the commercial brokers in Charlotte know that on any deal of size they can expect offers from group #1, group #2 and group #3. Why? Because these three groups bid on everything in that marketplace.

It is important to know your competition by market and by asset class and size. Certain buyers only look at value add, others only iron–clad Class A. Thus, it's important to know the competitors in your market(s) and know their criterion.

The Age Quotient

The age quotient for a multifamily asset has two components: the actual age and the functional age. One is no less important than the other. In fact it is often more important to know the functional age of the property.

In competitive markets age can sometimes become meaningless. When occupancy is tight, assuming usable amenities, the age factor can be diminished to zero relevance. A hovel in a major market with limited availability of rental units may rent for $2 a square foot (and much higher) as compared to .55 cents a square foot to rent practically new build units in a smaller, less populated or tertiary market.

The Actual Age

When reviewing potential multifamily acquisition candidates we always want to know the year built, or year of construction. This is our baseline data point that says much in a single number. Just by saying "year built 1976" we can make certain assumptions. One, there is lead paint on property. Two, if garden apartments, most likely all units will have only one bathroom.

Year built can also point to architecture. Year built also guides us towards the direct competition for an asset by quantifying the total number of units built within a certain time band. Example: 1980–1989. Depending on the locale and date, market data will tell us the total number of properties (and subsequently the number of units) within this age cohort in the market area for property X.

The Functional Age

Some properties get better with age, they really do. When this occurs we refer to it as "gentrification". The dividing point for what is "gentrified" is the amount of money put in the deal. Older property with completely updated amenities says that that people put money in– lots of it, to modernized older assets. Modernization can take the form of structural improvements (translated: big bucks) or cosmetic improvements.

Liam Neeson is a great actor. He tells a story about being on location in Europe. They were using an old bridge in a scene. He made a remark to a local about the old bridge. The local corrected him. "No sir, your movie is using the "New Bridge". It's not even fifty years old. The old bridge is over there– that one's four hundred years old. Americans often find this concept unreal, being in a country with such a short heritage.

To a healthy older person age is just a number. This applies to building as well. The age of a structure, while important, is less important than the functional age of the structure.

Always look at the actual age for clues to obsolescence and functional age for markers to forward–looking usability. Take both numbers into account when reviewing potential acquisition candidates.

Real Estate as a Store of Value

Recent volatility in the stock and bond markets has people turning to gold as a "store–of–value". Makes sense. Historically, gold maintains value, is a hedge against inflation and is transferable (weight aside).   When markets get rocky people look to invest in hard assets like gold and real estate.

Is multifamily a gold alternative?

The short answer is no. Of the various asset types within real estate multifamily is a favored investment. Can multifamily investment property be a "store of value"? Real estate, in terms of investment allocation theory, is not a replacement for gold but it generates certain benefits, namely income.

Gold is a defensive investment. Multifamily can be an offensive and defensive investment; defensive against inflationary occurrences and offensive as a current income generator.

As financial markets have increased in sophistication (with the use of margin accounts, derivatives, spiders, etc.) gold is in many instances just one more piece of paper in an investment portfolio. The vast majority of individuals that own gold have never held a single ounce in their hand.

Direct real estate ownership is different from gold ownership. Owning un–leveraged income producing real estate can provide a stable source of current income. Presuming the asset is in a quality market and insurance is maintained, short of a catastrophic event, you own it forever (forever in this instance being multi–generational).

Multifamily real estate is not a replacement for gold as a store of value. As an investment vehicle, multifamily does, however, offer some of the same positives as gold; as a hedge against inflation and as a store of value via being a hard asset. There are thousands of passive multifamily real estate investors that will attest to this.

 Thus, while multifamily is not a replacement for gold, it is an alternative investment with some similarities to gold when purchased without debt.

How to Read a Rent Roll (8 Ways to Sunday)

Following are eight ways to measure financial outcomes from the rent roll. There are numerous metrics to value a multifamily asset from revenue per square foot to replacement value. This writing is focused on the rent roll and various means to measure the quality of the income stream derived from the existing, in–place tenant base.

How Much?

We have many friends in various aspects of the multifamily business, some focus exclusively on acquisitions. One of my friends is notorious for saying "how much"? The question is unrelated to asking price. His real question is "<u>how much</u>" income is reflected in the rent roll and is this a valid number. Most focus on Net Operating Income (NOI). My friend targets valuing the quality of the income stream.

Here are eight ways to read a rent roll with an eye towards determining stability of the tenant base. The objective is to provide insight into the stability of the asset by knowing the financial reality associated with the income stream from multifamily assets.

Baseline Data. When beginning a review of the rent roll ask for two copies; one for the current month and one for the same month from the previous year (two years if you can get it). Our objective is to obtain a baseline; to determine those tenants that are on the rent roll in the current month and those removed.

Turn 'n Burn

Turnover. While a nice catch phase, in our business increases in turnover means we are burning cash. With the baseline data we can now determine turnover and inquire about the fate of those tenants no longer on the roll. What became of them? Each person previously on the rent roll was a paying customer and we are very interested in their fate. What happened that they are no longer a paying customer? Inquiring minds want to know. Most often, its standard stuff (the usual suspects) like job change, moving from the area, down–sizing, etc. For purposes of this analysis assumption is a very bad word. We really do want to know.

Revenue and Revenue Growth (Rent Growth). Minus the layered view of revenue including Gross Potential, less vacant, less concessions, plus utility income, plus garages... yada yada. How much RENTAL REVENUE was obtained for the current month versus for the same month one and two years previous? Without the "yes buts'" and "variance" stances, we are at the moment only attempting to determine the amount of rental revenue received for the most recent full calendar month.

Renewals and renewal rates. Renewals are the cornerstone to stability. What is the year–over–year renewal rate? A number north of 75% is very good. High renewal rates converts to a low turnover rate. Low turnover converts to high gross margins and less turnover expenditures.

Lease Start dates/Lease end dates. This is separate and distinct from renewals. This category says much about the potential of un–locking value. What is the average length of tenancy? Is it 12 months or 12 years? Nationally, turnover is fifty percent annually. As we all know, turnover is a NOI killer. Reducing turnover through retention increases cash flow. Excluding rent–regulated assets, longer average tenancy represents strong future income. Longer average tenancy allows you to forecast out further into the future when projecting revenue and revenue growth.

Collecting on Collections
Collections Activity. Collections refer to only collections of rent– not any other category. We are focused only on the rent roll. What percentage of rents are collected as of the first of the month? What is this percentage as of the second and third of the month? Collections in the 90th percentile on the first are representative of a high quality income stream. When collections activity increases there is an out–sized expense, in terms of time, necessary to collect monies due. At some point (determined by management) it is

better to not renew the lease than expend the time necessary on continuing collections activity.

Late fee revenue. Late fees can be an indicator of future collections. This revenue is a mechanism to enforce timely payment of rent. The real target inquiry is to determine the quality of the under–lying tenant base. Once late fees becomes consistently high, say, more than three percent of annual revenue, it becomes a red flag requiring deeper investigation. Is this line item confined to a particular set of tenants or is it property–wide? Is enforcement of the provision uniform? What are the credit underwriting standards for new tenants?

Evictions Activity. Per the rent roll, how many evictions were performed in the last few years? What was the end result on each one; voluntary move once served or action necessitating legal fees? What was the cost to turnover evicted units?

Consider utilizing this exercise on all of the assets in your portfolio. This may bring to light some previously unknown patterns. For example, it may be only four or five tenants taking one full day a month of management time for collections. Knowing this allows for crafting a remedy.

Can you add to this list? Please let us know through your comments. Thanks!

Bonus! Item 9... Compare revenue per unit year–over–year. Consider this similar to the "same store sales" metric used in retail and restaurants. A significant measure of revenue growth is to analyze year–over–year revenue on only occupied units.

Chapter 2

Property Management

Property Presentation (The eyes have it)

If one hundred people were to drive by your property and make a verbal comment what would they say? Would it be positive or negative? When ten people see an accident seldom do all the stories line up perfectly, but when comparing all the information a pattern does begin to develop. The same is true for a multifamily property; over a period of time a property not only gains a reputation, but a certain level of standing in a community (for better or worse). I'm not referring to marketing or property management– just street level, drive–by, glance through the windshield presentation. What does your property say to the world that passes by your front door?

Property presentation is an owner's initial visual contact with current and potential customers. There is just no getting around an un–kept parking lot or peeling paint, over–grown grass or broken window screens. These items are examples of low–cost repairs that should be eliminated as barriers to entry for new tenants and to assist in retaining current customers in a multifamily property. There are of course two things that a multifamily property owner never has enough of; cash and customers (whether cash for cap ex or variable cost, and customers, even if 100% occupied, then potential customers on a waiting list).

There is seldom cash to do all things all the time even for property presentation. For starters make a list of items that would increase curb appeal. Then rank these items in terms of costs. Do the things that cost the least first and work down the list towards the more expensive items. For example, let's say there is a rusted cast iron gate leading into the courtyard that really needs to be replaced. For now, lightly sand and paint them. Example: there are over–grown trees in the parking lot that should be removed. For now trim them back. Example: there are thirty exterior lighting fixtures on buildings that are old and some no longer work. Find one or two suppliers that carry a long–standing product, buy and install two per month. Start with the most visible area's and continue buying two each month until all are replaced. There are numerous things a property owner can accomplish to upgrade a site without breaking the bank. Example: hire a college age person to pick up the grounds every Saturday for two hours.

When looking at your property try to see what your customers see and ask yourself if their initial comment would be positive or negative. Work on the negatives, accentuate the positives. All while not losing sight of the budget. Just another day at the office. What fun! Growing revenue that is…..

Growing Revenue in Multifamily: The Ten Percent Rule

 Often in a given marketplace competitive properties have many similarities.   Granted, they may not have the same look or facade, but rent rates are similar (revenue per square foot of occupied space, for example) amenities are similar; they are the same distance from job centers or shopping etc. A deeper look will often expose that tenants are coming from the same pool; tenants have similar job titles, educational levels and credit scores. Same, same and more of the same. The ten percent rule proposed here is not an exercise to keep management busy or to assuage any particular interest group. The objective is to increase occupancy, and not just through the continued use of concessions.

The ten percent rule states that you will consider any single change from the norm in up to ten percent of the units in a development.

The following examples assumes 100 units or more and that not more that 10 units in total are "in play" to unconventional offers.   The objective is to fill vacants, not change the character or viability of the property. Here are some examples on how to apply the ten percent rule:

Demographics. For starters– expand your demographic.   Again, not by lowering screening standards, but through identifying additional people who fit your tenant profile. This may mean expanding advertising into channels that were previously ignored. A simple example is posting brochures in senior citizen and community centers. This demographic is more transitional than ever before– and they have income. Some sell homes and move to apartments close to where they have lived for many years. Many are looking to downsize but not leave their long–time neighborhood. Not everyone over the age of fifty going straight to assisted living. Baby Boomers are active in their community and they have income!

Short–term leases. Most operators have no interest in short–term leases due to the increased turnover costs. However, when vacancy is persistent, consider offering a few units with short–term leases at a "ten percent" premium to asking rents.

Utilities Paid. A quick review of utilities history will tell you the average cost per month for utilities (electric, gas) on a specific unit size. Offer a single unit with "utilities paid" and adjust the rental asking price accordingly. Do not in any way lower your screening processes to fill this unit.

Free cable and Internet. On a per unit basis. Offer one or two units with "free cable and internet". For many properties this is standard already but for many others it is not. For many properties either the entire property is wired or it is not. Similar to other utilities, the cost for providing this service for one unit is very easy to determine. Consider it a loss leader that may assist in filling one or two additional units. Likely, over one year, the cost will be similar to one month free rent– but note the concession is granted over the term of the lease.

Furnished Units. Get quotes in advance from Aaron's Rent's or similar vendors for the cost to furnish a two bed with Living room, Dining room and bedroom furniture only. Corporate rental would require full kitchen and linens (full kitchen is too expensive for a one–off rental). Just stick to offering the furnishings only and perhaps a television. Buy the offered insurance and factor this in your pricing.

Subsidized rents. Most individuals and families that have vouchers are good people. Even if you have not previously considered accepting HUD vouchers consider doing so. There are thousands of families and people of retirement age looking for housing that have a voucher that cannot find a property to accept their money. This in no way implies changing your screening standards. It will require having an inspection and filling out more paperwork than usual for a single lease but accomplishes a public good concurrent with decreasing your vacancy. A win/win.

Our objective is, on a continuous basis, to increase rents and revenue while providing the highest quality competitive product we can to our customer base. On that note, be prepared to step outside of your comfort level. In these economic times, with occupancy below historic levels, management's best efforts to garner increases in occupancy may not manufacture positive results. As noted earlier, as everyone is continuing to target the same pool of tenants you need to be willing to step outside of the usual box.

When Rents Fall: Four Things to Do

In 2009 there was little if any pricing power for owner's to increase rents. The same holds true thus far in 2010. With historic high vacancy tenants have selection and can demand concessions, often in the form of price. Since the recession began in 2008 any rent growth has been hard–fought. The size of the shadow rental market has never been bigger and to remain competitive the core of our business requires retaining good tenants along with marketing for new customers. This should be an absolute focal point of management's daily efforts.

With current tenants (depending on the volatility of your local marketplace) small concessions can go a long way to securing renewals; $100 visa cards, Starbucks gift cards, etc. In today's economy even grocery gift cards are an appreciated token for their consideration to remain for another lease term. We almost always offer to clean carpets at renewal time. This "service" is a help to the tenant and assist in maintaining property value by increasing the longevity of in–place flooring.

Following are four things to do when rents fall:

First – Make no assumptions. Are rents really falling? How do you know? The most direct method for identifying changes to your local market is through *market surveillance*. If competing properties are able to obtain higher rents than your property (competing properties being of similar age and quality), and occupancy levels are similar, find out what concessions your competitors are offering. A few years ago a free flat screen TV was a big deal (versus 30 days free rent). It was the type of premium that may be offered to a quality tenant signing an eighteen month lease. Today people are more cash conscious and would likely take the free month or other near cash equivalents like a $250 Visa or gasoline card. The economic times are dictating this. There is no hard science to tell us why a similar unit will rent for $795 and not $800– but we all know the social sciences tell us this is true.

Second– Don't panic. Rule number one (but the second thing to do) is to: *Focus on renewals*. Taking care of current customers is the first step towards assuring vacancy doesn't rise further. Every renewal means one less unit on the market. Too many operators focus on rent growth at renewal to the detriment of the property. Rent growth at the expense of higher turnover is a losing game when vacancy is already rising.

Third– Determine a marketing strategy (based on the market surveillance) that will create incremental increases in revenue. Here are some examples:

- Offer two bedroom units as one bedroom by locking off one bedroom, thus, effectively turning the two bedrooms into a one bedroom. If your market has an over–supply of two's this will buy you some additional occupancy. This idea should represent a very small portion of available units while offering just one more method to boost occupancy.

- In especially hard hit markets, offer two months free with a fourteen month lease. The first and last month of the lease are the free months.

- Add basic cable for new tenants (for six months). It's a concession you pay for over time while securing a new tenant today.

Fourth– *Coordinate your efforts so that all on property and off–site personnel are aware of the urgency to focus on full occupancy and reducing vacancy AND the methods being deployed to address increasing revenue.* Sometimes this means rotating staff from one site to another to cross train. Weekly or monthly staff meetings with "good" refreshments never hurt. Meetings should be one hour maximum, but well planned to cover specifics.

The Most Expensive Space on Property

Stating the obvious is seldom an over–statement. It's the thing right in front of us. We all know it's there, we're just not seeing it. Or worse, we see it and ignore its existence.

The most expensive space at any multifamily property is empty space. Pick a name; vacancy, un–occupied units, empties. By any name it is space available for lease that is not leased. An apartment is a perishable commodity. When a cruise ship leaves port for the week vacancy is set in stone for the entire cruise. In multifamily, we have a stationary asset but still multiple "cabins". Every day of vacancy is a day of lost revenue that cannot be recouped.

Efficiency in leasing requires preparedness. To the best of your ability, all available units should be made ready, particularly assuming you have various floor plans, bedroom counts and square footage. This selection adds to marketability and choice for potential customers. Potential tenants want to see the specific unit they may rent (if at all possible) versus a like unit in another building.

Complacency is not an option. A proactive perspective is imperative. Well trained personnel are the front line defense to address vacancy and should be compensated accordingly. As the old saying goes it's difficult to believe that military contracts should always go to the lowest bidder. Competency is key. We don't want "Joe College" who graduated with a 2.5 GPA building missile systems given the opportunity to hire better qualified achievers. The same is true for leasing staff. Hire the right people with the right skill set to get the job done, not the least expensive person to hold a seat down. Train consistently. Compensate accordingly.

There are only so many hours in a day, operations are constant, existing customers require attention. How do we focus on vacancy in the midst of the normal organized chaos of multifamily management? First, if this is the business you are in, and then you already know <u>eliminating vacancy is the fastest method for improving cash flow</u>.   That said, aside from maintaining current customers (by starting the renewal process for current tenants 45 to 60 days before lease expiration to minimize future vacancy) all eyes should be focused on that precious commodity spoiling at the end of the day– vacancy.   After safety and servicing current customers there is no better use of management's time.

Interior Upgrades that Create Value

 Although the United States is a relatively young country our housing stock is aging, the multifamily housing stock included. Usually, acquiring existing multifamily properties, regardless of age, is less expensive than new construction. In other words, you can buy property for less than replacement value.

For smaller multifamily assets (those under Five Million Dollars) almost two–thirds of the market is driven by 1031 exchanges. Transaction volume had plummeted with the extensive volatility the world has experienced across financial markets making mortgage financing more difficult. (Stronger underwriting requirements will be a positive for the entire industry in the long run).

That said, an older multifamily property purchased today will likely require updating in some manner to allow the asset to continue as a competitive property in its marketplace. Following are some upgrade suggestions that won't break the bank while showing your customers and potential customers that you are a proactive owner.

First and foremost; cleanliness. It seems so simple, but this one category is an on–going aspect of running a quality multifamily property. Common areas, parking lots and windows should not detract from the experience of coming to or living on your property. Consider as a general rule of thumb; <u>one man hour of labor weekly for each ten units for general pick up and presentation</u> (excluding normal landscaping upkeep).

Interior Upgrades. Considering every year there are dozens of new products with hundreds of interior uses, find one or two that work for your specific multifamily property. Do not do what the "Jones' do". Do not do what you cannot afford to do. While you are competing against nearby multifamily properties, you are competing more specifically against multifamily properties of similar age, condition and price point. Here are just a few examples of low–cost interior upgrades:

- **Quality Paint** and creating contrast. While fresh paint is good, some color contrast with fresh paint is better. Consider adding a single accent walls to interiors with an off–set yet compatible color (offset to the existing color scheme). Be consistent with color scheme and finish. Unless you are attempting to create an art deco look, earth tones and soft pastels work best. For product, stick with one name brand. This assist greatly with maintaining color match and quality level. Professional painters have strong preferences on where to use glossy, semi–gloss and flat. Consult your local professional.

- **Fixtures: Flooring** – use "eight pound" carpet pad rather than six pound. Granted, flooring is not a low–cost upgrade. But, before automatically replacing existing carpet (because old doesn't mean worn out), consider replacing existing pad with new eight pound pad versus the "cheapest pad you can find". While I can't put a specific value on this, the cost differential is nominal and the increased longevity in carpet is noticeable. I'm not quite sure how to measure "bounce" but more often than not it is noticeable. We have in the past kept ten–year old carpet but replaced the underlying pad with positive results. Granted, the carpet had some remaining life. This doesn't work with 1970′s shag.

- **Fixtures: Floating Tile**. Using vinyl, or floating tile, or a similar laminate is not inexpensive – but consider the cost/ benefits of using this product versus carpet when carpet replacement is necessary. I submit that the cost of installing floating tile is about the same as installing new carpet. The difference being carpet may have a 5–7 year life whereas tile will provide a substantially longer wear. Therefore, the actual costs of the laminate are less based on increased life.

- **Fixtures: Lighting**. Just about any lighting fixtures over ten to fifteen years old will show signs of looking dated. Consider the look and operation of the microwave in your home today and compare it to one purchased in the 1990′s. There's just no comparison. Sometimes a single light fixture can change the entire look of an apartment. Consider upgrading kitchen and dining room first. Make sure if you decide to change out lighting fixtures that you have a solid supplier. There are few things more frustrating than starting an overhaul and having your supplier go bust half way through the project.

- **Fixtures: Plumbing**. Water saving will become ever more important as utility costs increase. Change or install low–flow shower heads and low–flow aerators on all sinks (including kitchen sinks). Multiple name brands offer products reducing water flow from 2.5 gallons per minute down to 1.5 gallons per minute. This is a significant savings when considering it is applied to hundreds of units. On faucets; which way to go here? Do you buy the $79 Moen faucets or the $25 throw–a–ways? We buy deals for long–term hold. So our perspective is to have consistency in product whenever possible. So if a property has a single brand name faucet we stock the same brand along with replacement parts. Not true for toilets, however. Here, we maintain consistency in terms of set–backs AND round or elongated bowls AND rating. The bottom line is anytime you can replace a 3.5 gallon flush with a 1.6 gallon flush this can save a few penny's each day per unit. It all adds up!

One of the advantages to all of the recommendations above is that they can be implemented over time. Consider starting with water–saving devices. In a 100 unit development, installing ten low–flow shower heads per week will take ten weeks to complete. This spreads the costs of material and labor over time while upgrading fixtures and saving on utility costs. Every little bit helps increase Net Operating Income (NOI). Every increase in NOI increases value.

Exterior Upgrades that Create Value

Exterior Upgrades – Bringing Cost Conscience "Freshness"

In your market the competition never sleeps. Assume this posture in apartment marketing and urgency gets to be real. You are competing specifically against every multifamily property of similar age, condition and price point. In the multifamily business there is a new opportunity to make a first impression every day. Every year there are dozens of new products with hundreds of exterior uses. Find one or two that work for your specific multifamily property. Do not do what you cannot afford. Here are just a few examples of low–cost exterior upgrades:

First and foremost; cleanliness. It seems so simple, but this one category is an on–going aspect of running a quality multifamily property. Common areas, parking lots and windows should not detract from the experience of coming to or living on your property. Consider as a general rule of thumb; <u>one man hour of labor weekly for each ten units for general pick up and presentation</u> (excluding normal landscaping upkeep). Cleanliness includes paying attention to: trash bins, windows, parking lot, elevators, weed control, common area maintenance, steps, and laundry facilities.

Quality Paint and creating contrast. While fresh paint is good, some color contrast with fresh paint is better. Be consistent with color scheme and finish. Unless you are attempting to create an art deco look, earth tones and soft pastels work best. For product, stick with one name brand. This assists greatly with maintaining color match and quality level. Professional painters have strong preferences on where to use glossy, semi–gloss and flat. Consult your local professional.

Security Lighting. Many municipalities (not all) will provide additional street lights based a written request from a property owner. Certainly, an assessment will be made as to the need, but for older property's where street lights may be antiquated or under–serving the area there is no harm in asking. The same may be true for parking lots that, based on age, may not have any lighting. Under the guise of public safely a municipality may add street lights increasing night–time safety. We have one property where the city added six pole lights on property. Our costs were zero for the install and we pay approximately $60 a month for electric to power these lights. The impact on the property was immediate and dramatic in terms of the increase "feel" of security.

Re–numbering/Re–striping parking lot. Parking re–numbering costs less than $10 per parking space. Hire a service for professional finish (this is not a maintenance staff job– hire a pro). The value added here is removing confusion. Re–striping adds to safety and can bring a big dose of gratitude for the ability to have good guides into parking. It's like getting a drink in the drive–thru; you don't have to have a straw, but not having one is noticeable.

Sealing parking lot. Yes, this is a capital expenditure item. No it's not really low cost. Whereby it may not be low–cost, it is compared to parking lot replacement. Depending on the market, costs can range from 10–20 cents per square foot for a professional contractor to re–seal. <u>Weigh the longevity value against costs</u>. The upgrade will be noticeable to all and add a "pop" value in terms of newness. Cost/benefit can be somewhat difficult to measure. Consider though that New York City just filled its' two–millionth pot hole under Mayor Bloomberg. People notice. People don't really want to drive home every night into or through a hazard zone. (P.S. Under "stupid pet tricks; do <u>not</u> re–number/re–stripe and then re–seal. Re–seal first!).

Landscaping. Seeds. Seeds are cheap. Grass seeds, seasonal flowers, bulbs with reoccurring annual growth. Spend a little on seeds and each year they will pay dividends in terms of curb appeal and property consistency. Secondly, it's one thing to push the envelope to reduce cost on grass cuts, but before your customers begin to feel as if they are residing in the prairie lands eliminate the issue and add one additional cut per month. Consistently counts. That's what your customers want most.

Pool and Pool furniture. A swimming pool is an integral part of your multifamily property. After addressing safety first, make it usable. Make it part of the experience. If it's just an eye–sore, better to fill it in and be done with it. Like ice in a beverage, the water should always be clear. Any and all pool furniture should be usable or removed. Umbrella's, while a nuisance, are a plus. Purchase inexpensive umbrellas (but structurally sound umbrellas) as they tend to wear poorly and have a short shelf life regardless of quality.

Why Toilets are Important

Toilets are serious business. As a multifamily operator, a single broken toilet (one that is running water continually) can cost $20–30 a month. Running water: bad. Old toilets: bad. Not less than once annually maintenance should go into every unit to search for running water. Granted, most units have central air that requires air filter changes. If so, this is really the best time to "listen" for water and check toilet flappers, handles and seals. Review water bills looking for month over month variations by meter. Look at trend lines in water usage over time.

From the perspective of a multifamily owner, inefficient toilets are the fastest way to flush money ever invented (next to 1930's boilers and 40–year–old water heaters).

Seattle Public Utilities through the Saving Water Partnership (www.savingwater.org) sometimes offers multifamily properties that replace old toilets: free toilets (Ferguson ProFLO WaterSense), or $100 rebates towards 1.28 gpf (gallons per flush) WaterSense toilets. Wow. Toilets must be important.

There is history here that dates before the Roman's as to the importance of waste disposal and how to grow a city. Waste being removed from the population center also reduced disease (The Roman's were the first to build public toilets in an attempt to keep people from"going" in the street).

Toilets dated from the late 1960's (of which too many are still in operation) will use 3.5 gallons of purified drinking water with a single flush... no matter how small the tinkle. More recent "standard" versions have brought that number down to 1.6 gallons and "low flow" toilets are now using 1.28 gallons. There are also "tankless" toilets now being sold and waterless commodes at travel and truck stops along our roadways.

As every government municipality known to man searches for revenue they are certain to turn increasingly toward utility rates for increasing public revenue in less time than it takes Donald Trump to comb his quaff. Water is an absolute necessity. As such, the squeeze to make it as taxable as possible makes it one of the most ripe targets for rate increases. What to do? Reduce water usage.

- Fastest method: install water efficient toilets.
- Second fastest: low–flow shower heads and sink aerators.

There is a balance here between water efficiency and "flush–ability", or rating. Ratings range from one to ten with ten being best. The last thing you want to do when installing a new money-saving device is to create another problem. Thus, use a quality product when replacing antiquated fixtures.

In operations its best to utilize the same product type for consistency and parts. Consistency matters. This is true for toilets, paint, paperwork; all aspects of property management. Name brands are not as important as quality and maintenance free operation.

From www.toiletabcs.com:

Gravity Fed (1.6 gpf, 1.28 gpf)

The most common type of toilet is a gravity–fed model, which relies on the weight of the water and head pressure (height of the water in the tank) to promote the flush. If you see free–standing water when peering down into the tank, your toilet is gravity fed. Duel–flush toilets are one type of gravity–fed toilet. Dual–flush toilets let users choose from one of two flush options depending on need: Users can push one button for a regular 1.6–gpf flush, or they can push another for a reduced flush using about 0.9 gallons of water.

Pressure–Assist (1.6 gpf, 1.1 gpf)

The pressure–assist toilets rely on air pressure within a cylindrical vessel, usually a metal or plastic material, inside the toilet tank. Air inside the vessel forces a vigorous, rapid flush. The vessel, along with a powerful flush, is a sign of a pressure–assist toilet.

Dual Flush (1.6 gpf, 1.0 gpf)

Dual–flush toilets give users two flush options: Tilt the handle up for liquid waste, which uses about 1.1 gallon per flush. Or push the handle down for a standard flush, which typically releases 1.6 gallons of water. Duel–flush toilets that have 1.6– and 1.1–gpf flush options meet HET criteria of averaging 1.28 gallons per flush or less (HET criteria for dual–flush toilets identifies the effective flush volume as the average of one high flush and two low flushes).

Landscaping: Minimizing to the Maximum

Landscaping costs money. Maintaining landscaping costs money. The old adage "anything worth doing is worth doing right" certainly applies to this category because doing it wrong can make cutting the grass and trimming the trees a larger expense category than is necessary.

Think before you sink.... plants into the ground! Your choices directly impact the cost of landscaping maintenance in the future. Sustainable landscapes are healthier and require less resources in the future (things like; money, time, water, brain power). The more time you devote to this mode of thinking at the beginning of planting, the less time it will require to maintain long–term.

Sustainable landscapes are becoming the norm rather than the exception. "Going green" is an economic decision. Whereas installing solar panels, for example, has dubious benefits based on a cost/benefit analysis, following the **Green Building Council's Leadership in Energy and Environmental Design (LEED)** can have immediate positive benefits to the operations of a multifamily property. From the General Administration Office of the State of Washington:

*The U.S. Green Building Council is a national consensus–based organization of government agencies, design firms, product manufacturers and developers. The primary product of the U.S. Green Building Council is the Leadership in Energy and Environmental Design **(LEED)** Rating Criteria. The LEED rating system is recognized nationally and internationally as the green building design standard.*

Suburban multifamily properties very often have green space equal to or greater than the land area covered by buildings. Some properties have courtyards, or in some instances landscaping is used exclusively at the building entrance. Regardless of the expanse, landscaping cannot be viewed exclusively as an expense because in many instances it is part of the physical and aesthetic value of your multifamily property. Landscaping can be a "calling card" in advertising and represents, for many, their first impression of the property.

Landscaping can create an aurora, a certain mystique that wraps buildings with a presence. A living space defined by its' surroundings

Think of landscaping in terms of "sustainability".   With landscaping our objective is to maximize the value of foliage to the property and its' inhabitants while minimizing the expense of maintaining same. Landscaping is labor intensive; therefore, the use of plantings that can reduce continual manual labor is preferable.   Choosing geographically correct grass and plants creates long–term savings in water consumption, fertilizers and expensive pesticide treatments.

In an article from Environmental Design + Construction magazine entitled "LEED in the Landscape" (Leadership in Energy and Environmental Design) by Jose Almiñana and Theodore Eisenman, Andropogon Associates, Ltd. (2003):

Landscape architects and environmental planners are uniquely equipped to facilitate this process of integration and should be incorporated from the beginning of a project. One of the early tasks of landscape architects and planners is to understand the biophysics interactions that impact the site and the experience of the user at a variety of scales.

Why is this important? You don't have to be a fanatical 'greenaholic" to have a sincere interest in minimizing our ecological footprint in and around our multifamily properties. If better planning makes for better sustainable, livable space along with improving our customer experience, then, I see minimal downside to implementing LEED. Granted, this requires scale (of sorts).

I recommend asking a local landscaping Architect or Engineer to review your property and provide a "conversational" overview of possible costs savings. A $5,000 investment in environmental planning may save your property $25,000 in costs over the next ten years. You don't ask, you don't get. Saving the planet can sometimes be profitable!

Lions–Tigers–Bears – Dogs–Cats–Birds

Most multifamily property owners if given the choice
would exclude pets. Pets cause property damage, require carpet
replacements and generally bring an odor to a place that would not
be there otherwise. Multifamily properties with consistently high
occupancy can get away with excluding pets. These are most often
found in twenty–four hour cities and high density submarkets. For
the rest of the country, excluding pets means sending potential
tenants to your competition that will accept pets. Knowing that so
many are all too attached to friends with fur and feathers what is
a sound "pet policy" in multifamily management? Here are my
thoughts.

For starters, a pet policy rider must be attached to every apartment
lease with a pet in residence– no matter how small the pet. No
exceptions. This provides you with specific actions to remedy a
negative occurrence (that is, if the pet ends up being a nuisance to
the property).

Managing this piece of your business must take into account
the safety of all tenants including children. We suggest limiting
the number and size of pets per apartment to not more than
two pets with no pet being more than twenty pounds. Yes, this
excludes many animals, but presents an opportunity to increase
occupancy by accepting some pets and their paying owners.

Dogs are people too (Don't tell Mom but no they are not). But
to many people they are family (my cocker spaniel and I share
the same last name). Often, they are more loved and better cared
for than Uncle Otto who is only allowed to visit once a year. In
winter. When the family is on vacation. Disposition is key with
dogs. Avoid a law suit by meeting the dog prior to accepting the
application. Most are fine assuming they meet size requirements.

Cats truly are from Venus even if half are male. Most
domesticated cats are just that– domesticated. It's the cat owners
that are sometimes problematic. Most cat owner's love and care
for their animals like family. The few that give cat owners a bad

name allow their pet to use the carpet as their litter box. Any carpet, all carpet– your carpet. And that's the end of the carpet. There is really nothing you can do to save cat soaked carpet. This is the primary issue with cats– a few non–caring owners.

Birds are cute, birds are beautiful. And messy and sometimes loud. It's hard to justify that they have a place in communal living apartments. But of course there are always exceptions to the rule. I'm no expert here. May I suggest if and when you have a potential tenant with a bird you've never heard of or seen, that you ask about its breed, size and age. Then do some research starting with a pet store that sells similar birds. Ask some key questions and fold this information into your decision making process.

Snakes – How do you find snake love? I'll never know. I believe in disclosure. But when it comes to snakes do you really want a sign on the apartment door that says "Snake"! Are snakes a liability? Absolutely. Lovable? I think not.

Monkeys. No. Property management should not include keeping up with the vet records for shots and vaccinations of a wild animal.

Lizards. I have no ideas here.

As for the lions, tigers and bears… they belong in the wild.

What Would Woody Do?

Toy Story is a great brand. Woody, the main character in the movie Toy Story, is an old–time wooden toy cowboy (albeit animated). What does Woody have to do with multifamily property management? Lots. Woody has many of the qualities found in a good property manager.

I like Woody…

Woody has a full life. There seems to always be a fire that needs his attention and personalities that need stroking. He even has a girlfriend. I wonder if he sleeps? What has Woody earned for Pixar Studio's? I'm guessing over one billion dollars in revenue from all sources. What a great role model!

What Pixar has done with Woody is a perfect example of how to build a property management company. Finding winning strategies and systems; focus, sharpen, implement and repeat. Buying an apartment complex without installing good management is like fishing with no hook! It all starts with people…

Woody has many of the same attributes we find in a good property manager. Here are just a few:

- a positive attitude
- good problem solver
- a people person
- pro–active
- thinks strategically

And, he never gives up (on people, poodles or plastic personalities). These are all positive attributes to look for in personnel considered for property manager.

Individual Manager versus Management Company

On–site personnel should be vetted by more than just the owner. Back ground checks are a must as not all people are who they say they are in this day and age.   References, validation of employment history and credit are all part of this process.   As some properties accept cash, bonding may be part of this process.

As an owner, you are entrusting an asset or group of assets to an individual or management company.   If to an individual, assuming assets of several million dollars, then your decision point on selection is critical. I say critical because if anything were to happen with that one person note that your "key man" (or woman) is the link between you, your customers (tenants) and the continued operations of the asset.   Now, they could do nothing more than move jobs without notice.   This nevertheless places the owner in the position of having to find a qualified replacement quickly.

Hiring a management company offers increased flexibility at increased costs. Very often, the trade off is worthwhile. Management companies come equipped with most systems already in place to take over management and hit the ground running. They provide an array of specialist for maintenance and emergency fixes. And when the site manager has vacation time there is usually another individual provided to step in during this absence.

Assuming the owner (you) are going to employ a management company, as with an individual, check references. Further, ask for a sample monthly statement and a short written proposal of how they intend to implement their management plan.   If your contact person cannot generate either document, move on and find a qualified management company.

Self Management

This can be arduous and time consuming. Property management can be a 24 hour job if through no other means than having to answer the phone at all hours. New Owner/Managers seldom recognize the time commitment necessary to be a proactive manager. Before taking this step consider the time commitment and create a contingency plan. Property management is not for everyone. If your favorite thing to do is NOT talk to people and NOT pick up the phone– that's a hint that you need to find a

Woody with the appropriate skill set to serve.

If a happy wife is a happy life (true) then a happy property is one that has a proactive manager to assist current and future tenants enjoy their tenure in residence living in your property.

My hero: Woody from Toy Story. He is my choice for what a property manager should look like in terms of his proactive nature and assertiveness. And if we could have WALLE (another Pixar character) for maintenance we'd all be further ahead…

The Power of Incremental Income

When we talk about how to buy apartments the focus invariably turns to income. But is there a way to "juice" the revenue side of an apartment community without raising rents beyond comparable properties? Absolutely. It's called "other income". Property management is charged with implementing this from a "solutions perspective" with tenants as most other income provides a service to your customers.

The vast majority of revenue from multifamily property operations is derived from rental revenue. Great. Good. Wonderful. How boring is that? Actually, it's wonderfully boring in a stabilized asset. Particularly if you can keep turnover down.

Some fees are absolutely necessary to enforce the lease agreement (like late fees). The lease is the controlling document for the vast majority of income; rental income. The lease can also gain and control other income sources.

Think of other income as a menu of services for your customers (tenants). Some will be imposed upon them for not adhering to the terms of the lease (example: late fees) while others are completely optional (example: covered parking).

Note that many "high yielding" multifamily investment properties will often have high levels of "other income". There's a reason for that. Sometimes having high "other income" is a testament to the property manager or ownership group. They are just that good and diligent about enforcing the rights afforded the Landlord via the terms of the lease.

In other instances "other income" is all late fees. Consistently high late fees, while looking good on the income statement, are a testament to the credit quality of the tenant base. And you can bet management is working overtime in collections.

When a multifamily property is for sale "other income" can have big numbers because an owner/seller is looking to bolster their Profit/Loss statement. This could be to represent higher numbers to a potential buyer. Good business? No. Happens all the time? Yes.

Beyond rental revenue, what other opportunities for revenue growth are there from apartments? <u>How many different ways is there to peel a banana?</u> Let's see….

Application fees. The application fee is usually a wash as the fee collected offsets the direct costs of obtaining credit information and completing employment verification. Application fees can be used as a "screen out" function or a concession. When struggling to get people in the door this fee can be waved removing a barrier to entry.

Late fees. Late fees in C–class multifamily properties can represent as much as ten percent of revenue. Of course, this is earned through increased time, energy and effort in collecting payments. As part of the lease, late fees must be enforced fairly and evenly. It's imperative not to play games or show favoritism. I say this both from a legal and financial perspective.

Pet fees. If your multifamily property allows pets, then there should be income from pet fees. Like application fees, this is not a money maker but an offset to incurred costs. And there will be costs. We suggest limiting the number and size of pets per apartment to not more than two pets with no pet being more than twenty pounds (charging by the pound is probably a bad idea).

Laundry income. This can be a major source of revenue sometimes representing as much as three to five percent of revenue. The industry has evolved to the point where there are divisions within commercial laundry companies that specialize in the operation and maintenance of laundry facilities on property at multifamily developments.

Internet & Cable. Some cable operators offer a percentage over–ride for delivering customers to their service. This can range from 2–10% of revenue. Every market is unique depending on the local competition. Ask about anticipated apartment–wide product penetration and if there are minimum monthly fees payable to the service provider per unit (occupied or not). This industry, as it relates to apartments, is bigger than laundry services. Shop around and compare service providers. There is an array of services, some simple and some very complex Take your time implementing this .

Parking. Parking is a microcosm of economics where scarcity leads to higher prices. In many urban areas parking is no longer a right but a privilege. As our housing stock has aged the ratio of parking spaces to units has decreased significantly. Apartment buildings built in the 1950's and 60's presumed one car and one bread winner per household. In the 1970's many cars were bigger than a standard parking space. Going forward, many two bedrooms have two roommates. And they each have their own car. Fees are market specific and can include any of the following:

- Off street, single space parking
- Covered Parking
- Garage Parking

On site storage. The storage industry is huge in America. Being able to offer storage at an apartment community is a bonus not only in potential income but a quality attribute to sell to tenants and potential tenants. They can keep their "stuff" close by.

Concierge Services. This can range from laundry pick up/ delivery to dog walking. Many concierge services can be out–sourced so that the apartment property is obtaining a referral fee from the service provider **RUBS.** This stands for Renter Utility Billing System. Similar to laundry equipment and servicing for apartments, this is an entire industry with many service providers to choose from.

As you can see, for apartment property owners, there are many alternative income sources to pursue in addition to rental income. Start with the one's you believe will be most utilized by your customers and expand accordingly.

Focusing on G.R.A.C.E

Relationships are key to any established business. The same is true in the multifamily business. With established relationships in place, you can focus on G.R.A.C.E; growing revenue and controlling expenses.

G.R.A.C.E Requires Good In–place Relationships

An apartment property manager cannot focus on G.R.A.C.E without good people in place and good relationships supporting management objectives.

I'm the proud owner of a quality multifamily property and I am about to leave the country for six weeks on a dream vacation. The day before departure my manager quits unexpectedly.

Fortunately, my team rounds up some good potential apartment management candidates from within our company and in less than a day we have selected a manager. Our new manager has "some" apartment management experience, this person is a sophomore but trainable.

Green is Good, Sometimes

I'm almost happy. Why? (Is it because aliens have landed and taken all of the highly qualified apartment managers back to their planet– no). I am OK with this because I know my new manager has some resources, namely other team members managing assets for us already.

Yes, I'm leaving the management of this multifamily property to a green manager– green as in a reasonable person but with limited apartment management experience– but I've got coverage. But what if, through these unforeseen circumstances, we just discovered the next 'super manager"???

Luck, Smuck

I do not believe in luck. However, I do believe the prepared seem to be a little more lucky than the unprepared. Our selected property manager is not lucky; this candidate is taking advantage of opportunity. No luck necessary.

So let's look at another scenario. I have ONE multifamily property and ONE property only. And, I'm the proud owner of a quality multifamily property and I am about to leave the country for six weeks on a dream vacation. The day before departure my manager quits unexpectedly. Crap! Now what??

Email hasn't been invented yet and no one knows what a "Google" is much less how to spell it. Blackberry is still a berry (or jam in a jar). Kids are still playing Donkey Kong….

Fortunately, through friends in the business (there's that "relationship" thing again), I find a respectable candidate. This individual was an apartment vendor that serviced the area. The candidate was "down–sized" recently because the vendor consolidated staff and offices into another city. The candidate is interested, attentive and has passed the background check.

My plane leaves in an hour. Emergency averted, what do I tell tell Barbara (or Bob)? What words of wisdom do I leave with my manager? I can't point them to multifamilyinsight.net . It doesn't exist yet.

Deep breath. Here we go. OK property manager, I have three points. Take notes. Focus on these three things:

- Relationships
- Growing revenue
- Controlling expenses

With established relationships in place, you can focus on GRACE; growing revenue and controlling expenses. Once I get to my destination, we will devote some time to items two and three. The focal point of my message to our new hire is to "meet the folks". Our customers (tenants), service providers and vendors.

Take your maintenance staff to lunch or bring them donuts/coffee in the morning. I want you to say hello to everyone you come in contact with on your property. Wear the name badge and "plug in" to the site.

G.R.A.C.E is good, Always

Growing Revenue and Controlling Expenses (G.R.A.C.E) is impossible without sound relationships in the apartment business; with customers, staff, service providers and vendors.

Last thing. I'll call you every few days. Here's the key to the office and master key, and some deposit slips. Listen to the maintenance guy. He's been with us for a few years and knows the property very well.

Call any time if you have a true blue emergency. Otherwise, just leave a message at my hotel if you really get stuck on something and I will call you back straight away. Please remember it's a six hour time change.

So what's the backup plan? Let's say two weeks into the job our new manager quits (yes, this happens). Now what? Presuming there is a central collection point for rent collections, have your accounting firm record and make deposits. Then. Cry for help. But not to just anyone. Trusted friends and associates. Notice here, I did not say family members (If family, proceed cautiously).

You're looking for someone that can show apartments, fill out a lease and schedule maintenance (the basics). Assuming there is no one to answer the call, and then consider a temp agency. Expensive? Yes. But with a high probability of success until your return.

Without good "in place" relationships, there is no time to focus on G.R.A.C.E. With good working relationships in place, the opportunity to focus on G.R.A.C.E. exponentially increases.

Consistency is Key

What does McDonald's, Starbucks and Folgers all have in common? They deliver a consistent product. The cornerstone of running a successful multifamily business is consistency in management– delivering a consistent product.

Note we did not say consistency in multifamily location, age or price point. Coffee shops come in all shapes and sizes, but if the name is recognizable, we seem to look past the storefront because we know what to expect in terms of quality of product. Does your property management company have a brand? Is it recognized for consistency in your marketplace?

Practice, practice
Just like doctors and lawyers, apartment property managers "practice" their craft. Perhaps you have heard the saying "there is a difference between having ten years of experience, and one year of experience ten times". Our industry is always evolving.

Best Practices
Best practices should include <u>customer service</u> as a cornerstone to success. Many companies focus on leadership training. This is fine, but not if it comes at the expense of company–wide training… the kind that keeps everyone on message.

Our people as "software"
What's the one thing you want from your property management software? Probably first; you want it to work. Software products are an interactive tool we use to better our proficiency and get things done. Property managers have dozens of management software programs to choose from for increasing proficiency. Our customers (tenants) have little if any interaction with this. Their "software" is the manager. Our customer's (tenant) primary point of interaction with a property is their property manager.

Relationship Management
Our customers, they absolutely need their relationship with the property manager to work. Otherwise, they can move on

to another property. Seeking not only a space to live, but a good relationship with management. This cannot be under–estimated. Quality management interaction with the customer makes for a higher probability of a longer term relationship with the customer. Longer relationships equates to less turnover. Less turnover equals higher NOI.

We all have our favorite coffee shop. How long until you found a different favorite place if "Grumpy" stood at the door for each order? Probably not long. Our property management professionals are the front line to the customer. Managers are at their best when they are authentic, not wearing their feelings, being professional and engaging. In short, offering consistent customer service.

9 Things Not in the Textbooks

In multifamily property management I believe many of the points presented in this blog will be true five years from now. Like the chart of a long–term investment, one day does not a portfolio trend make. The same holds true in property management. Here are some things I believe hold true over the long run.…

The property management business will never be any less complex than it is today. Imagine that you lose your cell phone and it cannot be replaced for a week. In the interim there's an "old" blackberry in the drawer… that's five years old. The effort it would take to remember how it works may out–weigh the effort to use it.… if it would even work on today's networks.

Property presentation is imperative. Property presentation is an owner's initial visual contact with current and potential customers. When looking at your property try to see what your customers see and ask yourself if that initial comment would be positive or negative. Work on the negatives, accentuate the positives.

Management training is important, but there is such a thing as too much training. There must be "spacing" (read: time) between training to allow for implementation of new procedures/processes.

Landscaping is an asset. In an effort to reduce costs, this aspect of a property is often reduced towards extinction.   However, if we were to remove all landscaping from all buildings we are removing their character. Making them all the same. How boring is that?

Controlling utility expenses must continue to be a focal point of every pro–active property management company. Not only does is save real dollars, it also provides job security as increased cash flow gives cushion for keeping/continuing with professional management.

Relationships are key to any established business**.** The same is true in the multifamily business. With established relationships in place, you can focus on G.R.A.C.E; growing revenue and controlling expenses.

The "other income" category will continue to expand as our industry derives additional service categories. Look to services being offered by hotels and extended stay hotels for clues as to what may be coming next in the multifamily industry. We are not quite at the point of offering "bedding turn down" …but it could happen.

Innovation begins in our 24–hour cities and spreads outward. Innovation often begins with the solving of a problem. In the case of fast–paced, high population cities, the problem is solving for a tenant concern or request. How many properties had wireless Internet ten years ago? If the "fix" has legs, then this same solution spreads throughout a property and then to other properties. This same innovation will spread to other big cities and then through the country.

Commodity costs continue to rise (wood, metal, fabric, paint). Be selective with installed fixtures to assure they have a "timelessness" to them. Over–ride trendy with traditional colors. It's one thing to have a "hip" leasing office, but inside units, traditional colors and finishes provide extended life and more value to owners.

Sam's Club Syndrome

As property managers we are directing the spending of significant dollars every day. Products we use in property management daily are common to have on hand. Be it a disposal, air filters or cleaning supplies; these are usually just a few steps away on property when needed.   However, there is a carry–cost with having too much inventory.

Sam's Club is a great place to buy in bulk.   But let's face it; most of us do not need three mega–jars of Ragu sauce at one time. The same is true for supplies inventory at the property level.   Whereas cleaning supplies are a necessity, procurement of 55 gallon drums of Simple Green is over the top.

Just enough, good. Too much, bad.

It's important to have inventory on hand, but not so extensive that **shrinkage** (stealing), **spoilage** (loss of use) or **functional obsolescence** becomes an expense category. Eliminating all three can increase NOI without raising rents or reducing service levels.

Example: every property needs 9 volt batteries for smoke detectors. They can be purchased in cases of 144. Staff knows there is only X smoke detectors on site and that the batteries last, on average two years. There is no savings here buying bulk (for a single site).   Most of this stock ends up walking off the property. Best to inventory properly as there is no savings in buying cheap batteries either as they will require more replacement labor. Small example, but it adds up.

Example: a unit sustains water damage. The low–man in maintenance is in charge and order's drywall– enough to do a small house. In a miracle of engineering, it takes 55 sheets of drywall to repair two walls. And "low–man" trucks off just enough to finish his garage or basement at home.   Thus, while "low–man" is in charge of the job, YOU are in charge of the property… this one's on you.

Divide and Conquer!

At the property level, from a bookkeeping perspective, in your mind's eye separate <u>Cap ex</u> from <u>regular maintenance</u> from <u>turnover expenditures</u>. Although we order material and supplies for each of these categories, where can we find savings? The line gets gray sometimes if supplies for all three categories are ordered from the same suppliers. Divide and conquer (!) these categories.

The American industrial revolution produced more goods in less time than any other period in history. Part of the evolution of production included delivery of raw materials "Just in Time" for production literally eliminating the need for inventory.

Now we are at a point in time, recognizing the supply chain is not perfect, realizing that some inventory is a good thing in case the trucks, trains and planes are late or stopped altogether for whatever reason. Thus, while I am pushing here for your business to be "mean and lean" on supplies, don't shoot yourself in the foot by being too light.

The last time I was "allowed" to order supplies at the property level I bought ten boxes of 30 gallon trash bags. Legend has it three years later that original stock has five boxes to go. So much for "just in time" inventory.

The best we can do is learn from our mistakes. Protecting the property, delivering revenue and costs containment is a focal point our responsibilities.

The X Factor: Promoting Energy–Saving Benefits

The Multifamily industry is a large user of energy. We buy heating oil, natural gas and electricity in Billion dollar increments. This year General Electric closed their last operating incandescent light bulb manufacturing facility. How many incandescent lights are operating at your apartment property?

A standard light bulb (with 20 year old technology) uses 100 watts of power to generate 100 watts energy output. Compact Fluorescent Lights (CFL) use 26 watts of power to generate 100 watts of energy output. Using CFL can create a **74% reduction** in power usage!!!

The X Factor

For property manager's this can represent an A–ha moment. For professional property management, promoting energy efficiency can be The X Factor in your marketing campaign. Are you marketing in–place efficiencies?

It's easy to say, well, many of our competitors are sporting Green seals on their front door and LEED designations. This is true. It's also true that MOST of your direct competitors do not provide ANY proof of energy efficiency.

While it is common around the country for property owners to pay some utilities, what's important to potential tenants is what THEY pay in utility costs. In a competitive multifamily marketplace every possible advantage presented can positively impact occupancy.

People Buy Benefits, Not Features

Discussing insulation "R–factor" can be confusing (and boring). However, being able to honestly share the average utility bill in your city/market is $100 while that same bill is only $83 at your property is of direct benefit to your potential customer. So while having an expensive, good looking light fixture in the dining room is great, make sure your tenant knows the property only installs energy–saving lighting.

Everyone has brochures, rental applications, and information on Rental Insurance. Ho hum. How about providing a full page of energy–saving related devices that your property offers. Here's an opening for you to build on:

At Main Street USA Properties we strive to offer the best energy–efficient apartment homes we can. All of our apartment homes have the following:

- *Double–insulated windows to keep you warm in the winter and cool in the summer*

- *Energy–efficient lighting with CFL bulbs*

- *Energy–Star (TM) Appliances!*

- *Energy–saving, high–pressure shower heads*

- *Energy–saving, high pressure sink aerators*

- *Programmable thermostats allowing you to save energy while away from home*

- *Extra–thick padding under all carpeted areas*

Only if they are true can you promote on–property energy saving benefits with sincerity.   What energy upgrades have been accomplished at your property in the last five years? Roofing, windows, insulation? New HVAC or weather strips?

Remember: people buy benefits– not features. Otherwise we could have devoted the entire post to the energy efficiency provided by caulk!

Creating Job Security

As a professional property manager our objective is to lease space at a rental rate that delivers yield to invested capital. No yield, no capital. This basic principle gets lost in the day–to–day. Investors are seldom altruistic. They are results driven.

Creating Job Security

How do we create job security for our management company? In part by focusing on our customer. Who is our employer? Is it the person who signs our check (even if direct deposit)? Do we work for our vendors, suppliers and maintenance staff? The tenant, the baker, or the candlestick maker? Sometimes it's all of these. However, our real employer is the property owner.

Granted, often the "owner" is represented by a wall of legalese and complex ownership structures. But at the end of the day every property is owned by an individual or group or entity that seeks a yield on their invested dollars. They are usually sophisticated investors. And they know professional property management is a large part of their continued success.

Capital/Cash/Equity

Investor/owners supply the capital/cash/equity to own the asset. And they select management. They have the right and ability to hire and fire. This is our employer.

One of our primary responsibilities as property managers is to keep apartments leased for extended periods while limiting turnover. This keeps owners happy and creates job security for the property manager.

Owners are relying on you to manage their apartments in exchange for a management fee. If you are not up to the tasks, they'll select someone else. Nothing personal.

How do you create job security? In part by delivering results that exceed expectations. Excluding references to the cheese always being moved, part of this is sharing measurable results. This can be done in part by taking advantage of every aspect of your property management software.

Delivering Reporting that Deliver

Too many property management companies deliver a minimum level of reporting. Income Statement, rent roll. Unit Expense Report, Cash Expenditures.

I'm not suggesting that you paper the earth (even electronically) but consider the depth of reporting available from your software and deliver up stream all aspects of operations that reflect on how your good management is benefiting the property and it's owners.

The not so surprising result is that ownership may retain your services for an extended period of time as they become accustomed to the high level of detail delivered versus other management companies in their employ. Even if everyone were using the same exact software, most minimize outputs.

Try expanding outputs– appropriately, and see how this endears you to owners. It may create a little more interaction initially, but the questioning will subside as the owner becomes even more comfortable with the fact they have a property management company that understands the assets in their care.

Along with this, remember to ask for a two–year management contract renewal….

Property Management: Top 5 Tips for Growing Your Career

A recent story on CNN noted that being a commercial property manager is one of the best 50 jobs to have with median salaries around $75,000. The rating further states our industry to have a personal satisfaction rating of "A" and job security rating of "B".

Property management is a well defined profession with solid growth prospects. Job growth projections in property management range from 8 to 18% looking out ten years. Consider industry job growth will mirror the rate of population growth; about 1% per year.

This is great news for current industry property management professionals and job seekers. Job growth, security and job satisfaction are all ingredients of a promising career in property management. But to win jobs, you need to stand out from the crowd.

Training and certification(s) are keys to unlocking these opportunities. Here are my Top 5 Tips for growing your career as a property manager.

1. Education and training are crucial. Property owners know the best method for securing consistent revenue and maintaining expenses is to have well trained people– they know this is a solid investment. With education you are creating a transferable skill set.

For maximum opportunities a four–year college degree or industry training is the right place to start. A major in real estate, business or communications compliments a career in property management. The real thinking time comes in before you enter the profession considering your personal career objectives.

Real estate, like law, has many career tracks. Finding one you enjoy is important for job satisfaction. First, identify those specializations that are in high demand, and match these with your area of interest. By doing this, you are providing yourself with maximum flexibility in the job market while first learning, then working in your field of choice.

2. **<u>Professional Designations</u>** in property management. Adding to your credentials sets you apart from the competition and confirms your commitment to the profession. Beyond a college degree, advanced training affirms your willingness to devote time, energy and effort to becoming a knowledgeable professional.

The best time to gain credentials is early in your career as this allows for greater increases in responsibility. More responsibility leads to a greater number of assets under "your" management. This indicates more people reporting to you. This level of responsibility leads to greater salary increases.

When considering designations, the right one depends on the size and type of property managed and whether or not your interest is in site management or asset management. Here are a few to consider.

CPM – **Certified Property Manager** is a professional designation awarded by   the Institute of Real Estate Management (IREM) and recognized by the National   Association of Realtors (NAR). This designation is the most established and takes the longest to acquire. It is well known and has a high level of acceptance industry–wide.

- ARM – **Accredited Resident Manager** is a professional designation awarded by Institute of Real Estate Management (IREM).

- CAM – **Certified Apartment Manager** is a professional designation awarded by the National Apartment Association (NAA).

- CAPS – **Certified Apartment Portfolio Supervisor** is a professional designation awarded by the National Apartment Association (NAA).

- RAM – **Registered in Apartment Management** is a professional designation awarded by the National Association of Home Builders (NAHB).

3. Be a thought leader. As your career and experience advance, the Knowledge, Skills and Abilities you have become a valuable resource. With time and age people expand their knowledge from 1. Learning to 2. Doing to 3. Teaching. And sometimes from training to "training the trainer'. Being in leadership, people will want to be connected with you. Embrace this.

With experience, consider sharing your knowledge with the talented up and coming professionals following in your footsteps. Sharing your intelligence can sometimes change the perspective and enhance outputs throughout an entire organization.

 4. **Incorporate new technology.**   Stay current. Be a first adapter. Be well read. The technology cycle continues to shorten. Seldom is there a full twelve months between new releases of… anything technology based. It is so very fluid. Many software programs are on a continual/automatic update mode. You cannot ignore this.

 Email may not be dead, but it is dying. Today we discuss social media and tablets, tomorrow these forms of communications will have "adapted" to the next cycle of technological rendition. Right now transitioning tenants to secure electronic rent payments is all the rage. This is not to say that technology should rule your professional life, but it is the "life blood" of making certain your skills are relevant in the marketplace.

5. **PM is a Global Business.** Property management has a presence around the world. With quality training and language skills the world is your oyster in terms of job opportunities. If you are mobile, consider taking the best opportunity that can be identified– anywhere that fits your fancy; London, Athens, Bahrain.

Borders are meant to be crossed. Get a passport and expand the job search to companies and countries that desire your services. As a subject matter expert in PM, your potential employers are coast– to–coast and internationally.

Career choice is very much like taking a road trip; no matter where you start, it's always easier to get to the destination when the trip is mapped out first. Choosing a career in property management requires interacting with people of every stripe. Remember to think twice and speak once. It is an engaging and rewarding profession. Once you have decided to make property management your profession… jump in with both feet!

Misperceptions about Vacancy

There is a misperception about vacancy. The presumption is that vacancy is bad. Not true. Eliminating vacancy is often a property management company's number one goal. Sometimes vacancy is good. Really. For example, vacancy (turnover) allows property management to bring lower revenue/under–market units up to current market rents. It's also an opportunity to improve interiors.

An Easy Vacancy Example

A tenant is $200 under current market rent. A renewal is offered with a $72 monthly increase (a 6% increase). The tenant declines stating the increase is too high and gives notice to leave. This unit will now be rented at market rents–$200 higher. If the tenant had remained, the twelve month rental income increase is $864. Re–rented at market rate, the twelve–month rental increase is $2,400. Vacancy is good.

A Hard Vacancy Example

A long–time elderly tenant living on a fixed income breaks a hip, has huge medical bills and is just barely keeping rent current. At time of renewal, while the decision point may be kicked up a few layers, the probability of a rental increase is limited. Thus, rent maximization is not going to occur on this unit at renewal.

Whereas it would be in the best interest of the property owner to request an increase (thus, in essence, forcing a move–out) most property managers will defend their decision to allow this tenant to remain at the current rental rate for another year until the person can recover from their medical emergency.

This is an example where vacancy would be good from a purely financial perspective as the unit would likely be re–rented at a higher rate. But in the end, it doesn't matter because humans are still more important than money and a forced vacancy is not the appropriate call. In this example rent maximization gives way to common sense.

Different Types of Vacancy

Significant annual turnover is bad, of course. It's difficult to make money at any property where annual turnover approaches fifty percent. One potential positive to high turnover is allowing an owner to perform needed interior upgrades. This is only good if the upgrades bring stabilization versus continued high turnover.

Vacancy is often seasonal. Generic seasonal vacancy follows the school year whereas families move during late spring and summer prior to school starting back in fall. This can be good for smaller property's allowing an owner to hire seasonal help to address turnover while not having to staff year round. Consider then that not all vacancy is bad as the vacancy event can be utilized to make improvements and increase rents on units vacated by long–term residents. Yes, we all want long–term tenancy. Ideally, we strike a balance between length of tenancy and keeping pace with market rents.

Competition for Customers

Multifamily property managers devote a significant amount of time to courting new customers. We use all sources of marketing at our disposal to identifying viable leads, always seeking new and improved methods to target our audience. This post is about a single component. Marketing 101: identifying competitors.

The low hanging fruit in terms of knowing your competitors is finding other similar multifamily in your market, right? Simple. Yours is a Class B product in ABC market, find other similar property, shop the competition comparing amenities, price per square foot, age, parking, interior finishes, concessions offered, yada yada…

Alas, this is only one of the many competitors facing your asset. Following is a list of competitors to a multifamily asset.

1. **Mom.** Based on the depth and length of the recession many young people are staying home with Mom. Frankly, there is little you can do to compete with free; free room, free food and maybe even free laundry service. If you know of a strategy to compete with Mom, please let me know.

2. **Roommates.** What was once the standard one bed, one head is not always the case anymore. There is the live–in couple with a two bedroom now willing to 'sublet" their other bedroom to lower overhead. It's survival by any means necessary and this is another unit without a tenant for multifamily operators.

3. **Banks.** Certainly, banks prefer not to be home owners, they wish even less so to be landlords. Consider those with huge concentrated inventories. Whereas renting houses is out of their comfort zone, in some instances any rental income is good rental income to deflect the carry costs. This segment represents thousands of single family homes rented, therefore competing with multifamily for tenants.

4. **Motels.** Any city of size has these, they are the outlier places where a person or family can rent a one room hotel for $189 a week. Granted, sometimes the location may be suspect, but hey, for $800 a month and the option of leaving at any time these dwellings are a competitor to some multifamily assets.

5. **Foreclosures.** I'm excluding the shadow rental market here (although this is a segment of that). I'm referring to squatters. A disparaging term for good people that purchased a home in good faith only to see all of their equity disappear in the housing market collapse. Here is the best example as told by William Wheaton of MIT.

There are not less than three million homes in the United States where home owners have lost all or most of their originating equity. This equity is not coming back. In places like Florida it can take over a year for a bank for foreclose. Thus, there are thousands of "home owners" in Florida that if they so chose, could live in their same house free for a year.

This should make any multifamily owner shiver. For those thinking "we have tons of foreclosures in my market– why don't we have more traffic"? Because there are no concessions you can provide that competes with free housing for one year. My point is that as a property manager, when identifying competitive properties in your marketplace, consider also the number and type of foreclosures occurring.

What are some other competitive sources to multifamily assets? Please add to the list with your comments and I will revise this post to add your suggestions.

Multifamily: A Crowded Trade

A crowded trade is when too many dollars are chasing too few goods. Multifamily acquisitions is a full time profession for some and part time past time for others. Recently, both camps seem to be working full time making for a crowded traded in multifamily. But for how long?

Chasing Yield, Finding Yield

When people chase yield, they chase yield any place they can find it. In 2010, junk bond yields hit 20%...for a season. And then the herd moved on to municipals as they "seemed" safer with less volatility.

Think of the recent IPO of LinkedIN where some were paying 100 times next year's projected earnings. How can that possibly have any basis in reality?

The story is similar in the multifamily asset class. Multifamily had the best yields of any real estate in the last year. This increased interest and brought in more investors. Cap rates started compressing even as mortgage rates plummeted.

As interest in multifamily increased investors took note of the various means for capturing yield with income property via property owning REIT's, Mortgage REIT's, Private REIT's, partnerships and direct investment.

Often, for the retail investor, direct property ownership has too many strings attached. It's much easier to open a quarterly statement and read about the polished happenings at your property rather than contemplate the potential of late night calls about backed up plumbing. I simplify, of course.

The Professional Class

What alternative exist between owing shares of a public company and having direct responsibility for property management? Consider the alternative between these two extremes that is the professional class. This entails engaging multifamily professionals to manage multifamily properties professionally. Not a new concept, of course.

Keys to Success

For investors able to acquire assets with low leverage this is a viable (and profitable) alternative to passive investment in real estate that may deliver higher yields than more passive investment alternatives. There are two keys to success; professional property management and reasonable leverage.

Direct ownership does not fit for everyone. Here is a simple exercise. For sake of example, prior to placing one million dollars into a real estate fund, compare this to buying a two million dollar multifamily asset with one million cash down payment. The results may surprise you. Granted, the investor is exchanging geographic and property diversity for yield.

The decision point is determining if the differential in yield is wide enough to select direct property ownership versus public investment alternatives. Seek professional counsel.

Seven Reasons Why Rents are Rising

The recession that began in 2008 is the original cause of recent nominal rent rate growth. I do not believe, however, that rental rate increases will remain at last year's slow pace of increase. Rents are rising. Following are seven reasons why I believe rents will increase at a faster pace going forward.

1. The foreclosure rate, while waning, has taken significant housing product out of circulation. This housing cannot be purchased, sold or rented effectively decreasing the supply of housing.

2. Limited new construction along with incremental population growth is a spark in the tinder box waiting to explode. To maintain historic averages, in terms of the number of people per household, requires an increase in the housing stock. Otherwise, expect more people per household as housing becomes scarce.

3. The operating position of the Treasury and Federal Reserve. We will print more money (increasing M1) and buy more bonds (removing liquidity). This stasis, while maintaining low mortgage rates, continues to create uncertainty. In times of uncertainty fewer people buy homes.

4. Current interest rates are not sustainable. What's good for mortgage rates is bad for savers. While we, the consumer, are enjoying historically low rates, so are government borrowers. But there is no way, no how that rates can remain this low forever.

5. Home ownership rates are decreasing creating an expanding renter pool. More people looking for rental housing concurrent with limited new product is a crystal clear point towards higher rents.

6. Mortgage securitization is surviving on life support. Fewer people can qualify for a conventional mortgage today. And few firms are willing to take on the risk of bundling (witness

Bank of America's $8.5 Billion Dollars set–aside). No matter having the down payment in hand, Fannie and Freddie effective October 2011 have decreased the applicable debt service coverage ratio that defines how much a borrower can afford. Good underwriting all, but this will indeed decrease the number of families becoming homeowners.

7. Replacement housing is not being replaced. Housing that is taken out of service– for any reason, is not being replaced. Be it functional obsolescence, fire, flood or age. This is usually a small number, but it is impacting available housing stock. Yet another straw on top of the stack.

The perfect storm for significant rental increases is brewing. Shelter, food, transportation and health–care are all mandatory pieces of our modern lifestyle. Shelter is about to become much more expensive.

Five Tips to Full Occupancy

In multifamily property management, there is always more to do, but there are certain things that must be done. In the effort to maintain full occupancy, these five tips are in the "must be done" category.

1. **<u>Renewals!</u>** The straightest line to maintaining high occupancy in multifamily is focusing consistent attention on renewals. Ignoring this makes maintaining full occupancy near impossible.

2. **<u>Be Ready!</u>** Never show a unit to a potential tenant that is not ready to occupy. This includes "almost ready" and "gonna be ready next week" multifamily units. It's either ready to occupy or... wait.

3. **<u>Know Thy Competitors!</u>** Know where you can compete and where you cannot. Wendy's restaurant has tried many times to get in on McDonald's breakfast revenue. They just cant do it. Know thy competitors and what concessions they are offering in the present tense. Leasing agents should know amenities of competitor properties and how/where your property can out–perform. Example: older units almost always have greater square feet than newer product. Accentuate the positive!

4. **<u>Social media is a mainstay!</u>** Integration of Internet based advertising/media is a must no matter how small the multifamily market. The renter market is younger people (still). Young people are glued/stuck/fastens to their smart phones.... smart phones with connectivity to available apartment homes.

5. **<u>Two–way communication!</u>** Leasing Agents are far from order takers– they are the front line representing your asset. A potential tenant coming to your Leasing Office is looking for a place to live and insight on the lifestyle represented. A big part of leasing, then, is to dialogue and convey to potential tenants what they are buying.

This is accomplished best by creating two–way communication. Leasing Agents should be asking open–ended questions that draw information from potential tenants to better understand their needs and wants. This allows Leasing Agents to provide information on features and <u>benefits</u> offered by the development that meet potential customers lifestyle desires. People may look for features, but they buy benefits. The only way to know what benefits they are looking for is to ask.

Property Management: How to Move the Needle

As multifamily property managers, we have limited time to contemplate things we cannot change. There is a enough panic to go around, and around. Crisis. Uncertainty. Indecision. Each is beyond water cooler conversation and part of our real lives. Professionally, our focus should be on those things we can change at the property level; on how to move the needle in operations.

Other than job loss, and aside from those having to move down in price on their rent, I suspect turnover will slow as people hunker down during this current economic storm. Maybe this is just a wish (or pipe dream). We are creatures of habit, though, and these huge swings in the pendulum of governments and financial markets make people stand still for a time waiting for calm to prevail.

As property manager's of income property our two–pronged approach to improving operations in any market conditions must focus on <u>growing revenue</u> and <u>controlling expenses</u>. Growing revenue even in a sideways economy is possible. Consider any and all incremental pathways to revenue growth.

With respect to controlling expenses, consider upgrading technological systems (software) as a method of "sharpening the pencil" on expenditures. Synergies are everywhere. Identifying these within specific assets is where to find the payoff in terms of costs savings.

Using revenue of one million dollars, moving the needle two percentage points on revenue equates to $20,000. Moving the needle two percent on expenses (assuming 38% expenses) equates to costs savings of $7,600.

These are small numbers, I know. Multiply this at the portfolio level and they can be exponential. These small changes can reflect measurable positive growth in Net Operating Income.

In this economy where so many people are glued to CNN and Fox the progressive property manager will be in the trenches– growing NOI. And enjoying solid job satisfaction and job security.

Ten ways to find $10,000 on Property

When people find money it is usually in small increments like a jar of change or that lost $20 in an old pair of jeans. Following are ideas on finding $10,000 this year on property. Some of these ideas can produce $10,000 by themselves. Some may reduce costs and drop additional cash to net operating income (NOI). In multifamily there is no magic bullet, however, savings and revenue are sometimes right in front of us. We just have to keep looking.

Professional athletes know this well; it is not any one thing they do that makes for success, it is doing many small things well that culminate in high achievement. The same applies in property management. Presented here are ten suggestions for finding an additional $10,000.

1. <u>Answer every phone call</u>. Every phone call is a potential lease. Large Real Estate Investment Trust (REITs) have proven that answering every call can directly impact revenue generation to the tune of one or two percentage points per year. For multifamily assets with one million dollars in annual revenue this equates to $10–20,000 a year.

2. <u>Enforce late fee collections</u>. Adhere to the terms of the lease. Both Parties, property management and tenant, have agreed to the terms of the lease. The lease has a provision for payment of late fees. Enforce the provision.

3. <u>Thinking time</u>. Get ideas from those that know the property best. Have a brain–storming session with site personnel; management, leasing and maintenance. Make it fun. Have food! Really. No one knows the property better.

4. <u>Increase on–site coin operated washer/dryer fees by .25 cents per use</u>. Load factors are pretty easy to figure out. On 1,000 loads (wash/dry) per month a .25 cent increase generates an additional $250 per month, or $3,000 annually.

5. <u>Charge monthly pet fees</u>. It's common practice to charge a one–time pet fee at time of the original lease. An alternative strategy is to lower this fee (not eliminate the entry fee) and charge a monthly fee for each pet. This could be as little as $10 per month per pet. Size the fee based partly on the average length of tenancy. This will provide guidance on the total pet fees earned per pet per lease. On a 200 units property with 20 units having pets a $10 monthly fee converts t o$200 a month or $2,400 a year.

6. <u>Early termination fees</u>. Make sure each new lease and each lease renewal has a clause for early termination fees (if allowable in your state). This amount can range from one to three months rent for breaking a lease. This provision can add several thousand dollars each year to revenue.

7. <u>Review existing loans for re–finance opportunities</u>. The savings here can be significantly higher than $10,000 all by itself. This is one area where we prefer to stay away from the word "presume". Talk to real lenders and see what is possible.

8. <u>Utility Audit/Sub–metering</u>. Sub–metering saves money. A review of all utility expenditures is just good business. Here is one place to start: http://www.powerhour.com/propertymanagement/utilitybillaudit.html

9. <u>Energy efficiency review</u>. What energy upgrades were accomplished at your property recently? Lighting, Roofing, windows, insulation? New air filters or weather strips? What can you implement with the least costs and most immediate benefits? Install energy–saving lights bulbs... everywhere. And while we are all switching to CLF, check out the next generation in light bulbs: LED.

10. <u>Review all service contracts</u>. Few properties are out–sourcing the watering of plants anymore but there are plenty of other places to look for savings. Example: reduce mowing/landscaping service by 25% if possible without getting over–zealous. If the mowing crew is cutting the same two–inches of growth from three weeks earlier consider skipping a week. Or two weeks. If shaving mowing has limited or no negative consequences on property presentation, then skip. Consider contracting for a maximum eight to ten mowings in the summer months. Preferably evenly spaced. This equates to one mowing about every ten days.

Can you think of other ideas to add to this list? Please comment.

The Reasonable Person

Hurricane Irene is a reminder that bad things happen indiscriminately. Power outages and downed trees are no respecter of persons. This year, Tornadoes in Alabama and Missouri leveled entire neighborhoods. What responsibility does property management have when an entire city is on the edge of darkness? That of the reasonable person.

Like when a tree falls on a car on property, in my opinion, it is the responsibility of the auto owner's insurer to address the damage to the vehicle. It is property management's responsibility to address tree removal as rapidly as safety allows. This is an example of the reasonable person theory.

The reasonable person standard holds: each person owes a duty to behave as a reasonable person would under the same or similar circumstances

Whether hurricane or earthquake, if the property is deemed habitable by local officials, property management is charged with setting things back in order as fast as possible while working with insurance providers. And, as much as tenants want things back to perfect as fast a possible the process will likely be longer than anyone would like.

Encourage all tenants to have renters insurance. This is a good business practice. With extended power outages customers will often contact management about damage to electronics and food spoilage asking for reimbursement. Enacting the reasonable person standard, management is not responsible for Acts of God.

Have printed contact sheets for local government assistance agencies and charities. Consider that any assistance offered on property, such as food or blankets, is provided on a first come, first served basis until gone. If implemented, this policy must be documented as provided without favoritism.

Natural disasters are a perhaps no more prominent now than years ago with several big differences:

- We have warning systems that allow people to take cover in advance of pending danger
- Instantaneous news coverage that bring the events to our front of mind in real time
- Population density in big cities that is at historic highs

These factors impact the property management business. And while no single property is more important than any single person, we must use common sense and act as a reasonable person when addressing natural disasters that affect the property in our care.

Property Management: 5 Things We DO NOT DO

What are some things you do not do? Most activities in property management are relegated to daylight hours. Most of us know this. Alas, there is always that guy wanting to mow grass at midnight or something similar. My point is there are certain things we don't do.

In property management, we are on call 24/7. We have to answer every call (even the annoying ones). Some things can wait until the light of day. Other matters require finding the bunny slippers at two a.m. to make that call to on–call maintenance (while praying they answer!).

Here are a few miss–steps to avoid in property management:

1. Letting insurance premiums lapse. Insurance is many things. One of those things is necessary. Letting hazard insurance or workers comp lapse is just an accident waiting to happen (pun intended).

2. Allowing running water to run. Water is a menace to property. Like the seasons it is always changing and unpredictable. Anytime running water can be stopped do not delay. And standing water turns into pooling water. Seldom is this a good thing.

3. Turn away a paying customer. Just thinking about this makes me want to cry! Do all you can to retain this customer. Even if they cannot remain on your property, then send them to a sister site. Anything else is lost revenue.

4. Anything to do with natural gas. Anything to do with natural gas other than lighting a pilot probably requires a professional. This is no time to call your cousin to save a buck. Call a professional. Immediately.

5. Ignoring roof leaks. (See allowing water to run). There is no way out of this one. Any roof leak is only apt to expand– not contract.

Can you add to this list? What is the number one thing that you stress to staff to "don't do"? Let me know with your comments.

8 Places to Find New Multifamily Tenants

We live in an "on–line" world. The demographics of potential apartment tenants are connected through all the channels you already know about from Facebook to Apartments.com. Consider, however, that most of your new customers are from a very small radius, anywhere from one to five miles from your multifamily asset.

Whereas most may be on–line" this is a presumption as Internet connectivity rates vary significantly from place to place. And, for those that are connected, their search abilities also vary significantly.

So, we know many (but not all) of our potential customers are connected and we know most are from a radius close to our asset. What can we do with this information? We make sure our advertising mix has depth versus breadth. We want to have a high level of coverage close to the asset. This requires some 'old school" foot power visiting places close to property going to where our customers work, worship and go to school.

Thus, while it's nice to advertise in the newspaper that covers the entire city (making sure y0ur ad is in the on–line version), most of your new customers already live right around the corner. Literally. Here are eight places to look for new customers.

Craigslist. Craigslist still works. We place a phone number only and no email as email seems to attract too much "junk". Those that call, however, are usually good prospects.

The Real Wall. Not the Facebook wall. Just about every place of business has "the wall" where people place information for everything from "free puppy's" to places to rent. It's a captive audience, really. And for those businesses close to your property it can be a great place to find new tenants. The connection is that given the choice people prefer to live close to their place of employment. Well, help them out. Ask permission to place a flyer on the employee wall. This is where to start: draw a one or two mile radius around your multifamily property and identify any and all employers of size.

The Church Bulletin. Do a Google map of churches within close proximity of your asset. Betcha there are more than five. We have one asset within one mile of a church with over 5,000 members. Granted, it may be a stretch to advertise in the church bulletin, but any church with real size may have other printed material with sponsor/advertising opportunities. And the likelihood is high yours will be the only apartment property with a display ad capturing the eyeballs of these potential customers.

Community Boards. From the bingo parlor to grocery stores, people really do read community boards. And, just like "the wall" post at places close to your multifamily asset.

Cash Register Receipts. What makes this viable is the low costs and because they are repetitive. People tend to be creatures of habit so they do their grocery shopping at the same place every week. That means every week they will be seeing your advertisement.

Sponsorships. When it comes to sponsorships, most people think of very big or very small options, like Little League t–shirts or stadiums. Like all advertising, we want the most targeted eyeballs for our dollar. One place that is low costs and high volume is school newsletters close to property. Consider placing advertisements (sponsored ad's) in the local elementary school newsletter. This will be low cost and targeted. An elementary school with 400 kids has almost as many families and they are all right in your neighborhood.

Single–family "for rent". Depending on the size of your city, the newspaper apartment advertising section may have hundreds of listings. By comparison, in the same print version you will find only a few single–family homes for rent. If your asset is patio homes or duplexes, consider placing an ad in the "single–family" section clearly stating "apartment homes" (two bedroom with den and great view, etc). The intent is to provide your multifamily asset and potential tenants with another avenue for finding your property. This can only be accomplished with full disclosure to the newspaper classified staff. This works great for multifamily duplex communities.

Restaurants. Many neighborhood restaurants have turned their tables into advertising venues. These are very permanent so be sure to double–check your web address and phone number. The costs may be higher than other forms of advertising but the staying power and repetitive nature of the ad's make them a viable consideration. If the place is close to your asset and a mainstay in the community this is a win/win.

Property Management and the Amazing Affects of Coffee

Most people enjoy a good cup of coffee in the morning. It is the ultimate "me time" before we start our day. Just about every place of business (non–retail) has coffee and bottled water nearby during business hours. Why? And what does this have to do with multifamily?

Coffee is an amazing business tool. While probably overlooked by Drucker, it really is utilized across the world as a handshake, a welcoming comfort food. It says "stay a while". Why is that important? Let's talk groceries.

Retailers and Grocers devote significant people and resources to store layouts. In any grocery store of size there is absolute rhyme to the reasoning as to why milk is in one corner of the store nowhere near the bread, and one hundred yards from the nearest apples.

The objective is to keep the shopper on property and allow them to walk/move past added merchandise. Be assured every major grocer recognizes the correlation between the average number of dollars spent per minute in the store. For every additional minute a shopper spends on property they spend more money. This correlate to potential new tenants in multifamily.

What is the value of your coffee pot?

In multifamily, our "stores" will have a model unit if possible. This is a place for people to roam around, stay on property and get a feel for the place. Not all properties have a model, but we can have coffee. It is a business tool we have at our disposal to give people a reason to stay a while.

Can your coffee pot produce one additional lease each year? If so, how much value is that creating for your multifamily property over five years? Betcha that's a big number.

What is the value of one additional lease each year?

And, like with the grocery business, the longer they stay the higher the probability they will buy. In this case, they are usually contemplating a potential one year lease. This may be a $7,000 or $27,000 decision.

Give potential tenants cause to stay a while. Make sure the coffee is good. It may gain you one or two additional leases each year. Have fun determining your return on investment on that!

Multifamily Make–Ready's Made Easy

The best way to assure easy make–ready's is to have as few as possible, right? How to make that happen? With an earnest focus on lease renewals. Focusing on renewals reduces turnover. Concessions at lease renewal are almost always less expensive than turnover expenditures. Be it carpet cleaning, painting an accent wall or a few new light fixtures, any of these require less cash than a full make–ready. Considering potential days vacant they are a bargain.

What else makes make–ready's easy? Preparation. Preparation is having a handle on the resources required to perform make–ready's thirty days prior to requiring those resources. By resources we mean lining up labor, material and equipment. Simple, right? But where to store that roll of carpet?? We'll get back to that. More importantly make–readys begin with the lease renewal process.

The backbone of being prepared for make–ready's is in the leasing renewal process. Lease renewals are your "leading indicator" to up–coming turnover, right? Without pro–active renewals it is impossible to prepare for pending turnover. Renewals cannot be taken for granted. Beginning the renewal process 90 days prior to the end of the lease term, anymore, is becoming standard operating procedure and represents the best tool in preparing for make ready's.

Back to carpet. Most major metro's have a selection of vendors on carpet. Inquire with yours about their ability to store rolls for you (whole or part) for free. The caveat is that they will want you to use their installers. Well, if you are doing this anyway this is a win/win. You obtain free carpet storage and your vendor knows you think of them as your "one stop shop" for carpet and installation. This is built–in work for the vendor going forward as the roll is used up.

Be fast, but do not be in a hurry – John Wooden (Legendary UCLA basketball coach)

Few property management companies keep much inventory on hand anymore. Many of us consider Home Depot and Lowes as our inventory warehouse. But when it comes to turnover a lack of inventory can add days to units being off–line. So stock certain items <u>in advance</u> because, as you know, most properties in your market area are in turnover mode at the very same time. Consider utilizing a vacant unit for temporary storage.

Let me repeat; consider utilizing a vacant unit for temporary storage– only. If there is any chance this "temporary" staging/ processing area will become permanent just pass– don't do it. Now, assuming use as a temporary staging/processing area is available then only place boxed, non–liquid and light weight materials here. No paint, no HVAC units. Items include; blinds, air–filters, plumbing and light fixtures (boxed),

The positive outcome to having a systematic make–ready structure is minimizing unit down time, or off line days per unit. Most professional management software will have a report option for tracking this.

Then there is the paperwork. Any and all advanced documentation in hand will decrease days off line. Performing a pre–exit walk– through when the tenant notifies of move out places your team in position for quick turnovers.

Electronic files, paper files, personnel– Oh My! It is true, your best maintenance guy can fix anything. Even so, getting him to put down the paint brush and plumber's putty to type a few words into an iPad is very unlikely. For some processes paper is still our best friend. Having a record paper record of turnovers is important, albeit a two–step process; converting paper records into electronic documentation. It is a worthwhile step to avoid duplicity and track inventory.

Chapter 3

Demographics
and
Market Analysis

Why Multifamily is about to have a Good Decade

In 2010 there are over 300 million people residing in the United States. Based on the severe financial stresses these past eighteen months we have eight million fewer jobs, but no fewer people. Christmas sales were slightly higher in 2009 than the year before, auto sales are stabilizing, the savings rate is increasing, and jobs losses are decreasing. And the population continues to climb. It seems regardless of economic happenings people continue to have babies. And babies, and their siblings, need housing.

We've heard much in recent months about the shadow rental market and how foreclosures are competing with multifamily for renters. Remarkably, multifamily defaults have not skyrocketed throughout these massive shocks to our financial system. Multifamily properties remain stable, continuing to provide housing for nearly a quarter of the nation's population. And this too shall change. There is a silver lining to many of these occurrences. One of them is that multifamily apartment owners are about to have a very good decade.

While we were all glued to our 'tubes" watching MSNBC and FOX describe the end of the world as we know it a few things didn't change; people continued to consume food and shelter. And have babies. In the last eighteen months construction starts have fallen off a cliff to an annualized rate of 600,000 units. That level of construction was fine with a national population of 180 million people, but significantly under our current (and future) housing needs. Also, along the way, credit has disappeared. As most have noticed obtaining a mortgage is no small task in this market.

Less access to credit means fewer home owners. Fewer home owners mean more renters. And even though our population is aging the age quotient of renters is expanding as there are now more age 50+ renters than ever before. Adding these factors to the last two years of historic low new construction and we submit that multifamily owner's are about to have a very good decade.

Who is in Your Tenant Pool?

In the last twenty years the renter pool has expanded well outside the age cohort of twenty something. Renting as a lifestyle choice is very much a common happening today. As housing affordability has decreased in recent years more families have continued as renters.

Even though affordability has returned (somewhat) with lower interest rates, home ownership numbers are not increasing as jobs continue to be scarce and loans difficult to come by.

When looking to buy apartments the bigger the qualified renter pool the better

Seniors, young families and working professionals over the age of thirty, all are now mainstays of the renter pool representing a demographic who rent as a lifestyle. There is certain rental housing targeted for specific tenants; students, seniors over the age of fifty–five, etc. Everyone else should be in your tenant pool. Who is your target audience?

- Most everyone is aware of the non–discriminatory laws that we must all abide by. But can you stretch? Many older properties were not constructed for handicap access so they do not have to offer accessibility. But do you have a unit that can be converted for this use? Imagine how many people you can add to your tenant pool by offering a handicap accessible unit. Granted, it's difficult to change door sizes, but sometimes just a few changes can increase the possibility of a handicap person selecting your property. Handicap rails in the bathroom for example. Or a doorbell with lights for a non–hearing person.

- Many owners have a no pet policy. There are many reasons for this and I would submit if you do not have to open up your property to pets then do not. But, right now we are looking for tenants to increase our pool of potential customers to fill our units. So consider making some units available for pets – small pets. Pets under ten pounds. Make sure to add a Pet Rider to the lease and spell out that if the pet becomes a nuisance to neighbors that it cannot stay. There are so many pet lovers in the world now is not the time to exclude them from our renter pool if you can possibly accommodate them. And have reasonable, onetime, non–refundable pet fees. There is no reason to put this out there and take it away with high fee barriers.

- Today, if you are age fifty you can join the AARP. Apparently, a single gray hair qualifies a person as being a senior citizen. These working professionals are not hanging out at the "center" quite yet, but they do need housing. They go to plays, they work out at the gym. They have investments that create income to subsidize their wages. As renters, they want a hassle free environment where maintenance is timely and late night noise is minimal. While this cohort is not significantly active in electronic social media (they still buy newspapers and magazines) they bring income stability to a property as their length of stay is often longer than the average renter. Find out where they are in your marketplace.

Please note these suggestions for adding to your rental pool do not include lowering screening standards. There is no reason to increase occupancy AND turnover for non–payment. That's a vicious cycle to be avoided. Do some brainstorming and add to this list. Every additional paying customer is one less vacant unit adding to NOI.

The Declining Significance of Home Ownership

In the last two generations home ownership has become a mainstay part of the American Dream. Unfortunately, so has ever–increasing complexity in the financing of this dream. Home ownership is a privilege, not a right. This privilege is open to most willing to sacrifice savings (down payment dollars) and sign a long–term note (mortgage) to finance the balance of the purchase price. The "invention" of the thirty–year mortgage did more to increase home ownership rates in the U.S. than any other modern financial instrument until the creation of subprime mortgages. Alas, progress is not always forward. Most people today know that your principal residence is not an automated teller machine to be tapped for every whim.

As many families have learned in recent times, home ownership is not always in their best interest. Is there really such a thing as "negative equity? Yes. There are scores of people wishing they did not know the definition. When the percentage of the population owning homes was peaking at seventy percent, foreclosure rates were soaring. It wasn't that too many people had become home owners; it was that too many had people become home owners through the use of exotic mortgage products. Now that mortgage products have retreated to more standardized underwriting, home ownership will return to its historic norms of around sixty–seven percent of the population.

As the home ownership bell curve returns to normal this will increase the renter pool along with favorable demographics and, for some, an inclination to remain as renters for life having been stung by various financing instruments (subprime mortgages) and foreclosure. Multifamily owners should consider foreclosure on a credit report as a factor when considering a potential tenant, but not use such as an automatic exclusion. Similar to medical bills that can decimate a credit rating, a single mistake of signing for a dysfunctional mortgage product should not exclude an otherwise quality tenant (all other things being equal). Consider the circumstances, consider the times.

Home ownership is a worthy pursuit. Families should consider the nature of the commitment and affordability when considering a purchase, using prudent levels of leverage and considering sustainability. It's not for everyone though. Renting as a lifestyle choice will continue to be a consistent alternative for nearly one–third of the population.

Where are my Tenant's and are they Coming Home Soon?

Where have all my renter's went? They were here just a while ago. My multifamily property looks at its best. Management is doing all the right things. Heck, we even painted the sign and checked to make sure the phone was plugged in. Now what? First, be ready for their return. Don't become so complacent that you leave units off–line for extended periods without review. This only causes more harm in the long run as shuttered units develop additional problems (complacency begets complacency). The biggest factor in timing a measurable increase in traffic will correlate with jobs. Jobs jobs jobs.

Assuming your potential customers are not completely avoiding your multifamily asset because of poor presentation, mis–management or missing windows; where are they? At the moment they are home with Mom or doubling up with that high school friend to save money. Most are looking for jobs. Many are under–employed maintaining part–time work while waiting for the jobs market to strengthen. I know of one couple that divorced but still live together because it was the most cost–effective thing they could do to maintain their lifestyle during this recession.

In–migration may be taking a break during the recession but so has construction. The level of residential construction has slowed so much that as demand begins to pick up the tide will eventually turn; first to normalized historic occupancy, then surpassing this level until such time as construction activity makes significant strides. The question is how long will it take to burn off the current "excess" inventory that has created the massive shadow rental market from single family. My estimate is no time soon. When people begin to "unpack" from doubling up, multifamily vacancy will decrease and rent growth will return but only moderately. For that to happen we need consistent GDP growth above three percent (3%) and job growth of 100,000 jobs per month. These are nominal growth rates that would lead to greater stabilization and not exponential increases.

When things get this tight the rental market becomes a zero sum game. Since there are more multifamily units than people to rent them it's like a round of musical chairs with too many chairs; even when everyone gets a seat there are still seats remaining empty. As there is an excess in capacity (at the moment) your customer's have more alternatives than just about any time in the past ten years. Many of your potential customers are shopping– and shopping hard. Can you answer the following questions with a few minutes' notice?

- Do you know your competition? What multifamily properties, specifically, is your asset competing against?

- Are your concessions competitive or better than competitive multifamily properties? There are no awards for second place.

- What is your cost per square foot compared to competing properties of a similar age and with similar amenities?

- Have your reviewed your advertising venues and response rates? Do you have a website tie–in to your local advertising?

If you can afford to do so, continue with cosmetic upgrades even with the currently disproportionate vacancy. You will be better prepared to absorb new tenants and not be in hurry–up mode to accommodate them. Use a checklist format for reviewing ready units. Consider adding an accent wall in the living room (a single wall painted in an offset color to the rest of the apartment), upgrading light fixtures and plumbing fixtures if they are dated.

Prepare to be competitive while controlling costs. Growing revenue while controlling costs has the most direct positive impact on Net Operating Income (NOI). Growing NOI is growing asset value.

Location IS NOT Everything

Location, location, location. Blah, blah, blah. So tell me something I don't know. Did you know the people living and working close to a multifamily asset are as important as the asset itself? When looking for apartments to buy, how much time does your team focus on the demographic profile of the current and future tenant base?

Demographics rule!
The outer ring in the multifamily space (tertiary markets) can be just as competitive as 24 hours cities– assuming quality demographics. When reviewing potential acquisition candidates, I focus as much on the demographics of the people living in the area as I do the specific building(s) or development.

Income, average age, household size, type of employment, level of crime against people and property– these are factors weighing on the quality of the acquisition candidate under consideration. These categories, collectively, provide high level determinants of future value of apartment assets.

Buildings alone do not a building make
While location is a large component in the multifamily buying decision, it is by no means the sole decision point. What "surrounds" an apartment complex is just as important as the building(s) itself.

No doubt you've seen advertisements for property's that say "walk to train". Invariably, some of those units are eye level with the train on raised tracks. Others are a half a mile away. I'm not talking about "advertising" or property positioning. I'm referring to property placement with respect to proximity of surrounding dwellings, businesses, services and jobs.

Not to pick on Michigan, but most people know the state is losing population. This fact makes it difficult to buy Michigan markets recognizing the going–forward demographic will be an aging population with fewer young families. Recognition of weak market demographics makes submarket selection and analysis all the more important.

People, Places, Parking

Have you ever driven by a great looking restaurant and decided to try it only to find NO parking. Isn't this disappointing? What about going to a bagel shop that is out of cream cheese? What's the point. Granted cream cheese is not an absolute necessity but if you wanted it that morning then, well, you wanted it.

These are two examples of ancillary, but necessary, articles that diminish the experience of a place. In the first example the experience is eliminated altogether not because of location but because of access to location. In the bagel example even if the customer buys, they are still disappointed in their buying decision. The same holds for property placement, if enough factors surrounding a site disappoint potential customers (tenants), well then, the place itself can be deemed as disappointing.

Property investing is not a passive activity. A viable multifamily asset has many factors in its favor from quality of construction to good access. One of the greatest strengths of a particular asset we manage is not the buildings on site, but the tenant base. Average turnover in apartments is 50% annually. In this particular asset, turnover is less than 25% each year. This one fact adds significant value to the underlying asset as turn costs is substantially lower than similar properties.

Think of demographics as the tires and wheels of a car. A car cannot move without four tires, evenly balanced. Positive demographic attributes, like tires, assist in carrying a property forward. When maintained well, they can last long into the future.

Anatomy of a Submarket

The number of existing and proposed housing units in an area and their impact on rent growth is directly correlated to population and income. But population and income growth where? The "where" is in the submarket that an apartment property competes– the area defined partly by competing properties with similar attributes.

A submarket is a geographic area defined by streets, natural barriers and the specific properties in which a property is in competition for customers

Once the submarket is defined, a multifamily property owner or management company has a very solid view of the population, income and competitive properties affecting a give apartment asset.   Seldom is this area square or round. Nor does the shape or size follow census tracts or block groups.

Making a determination about population growth and income, and aligning this information with the number of housing and multifamily housing units will provide guidance of future vacancy and rent growth.   These factors have significant impact on value.

 The funnel approach to identifying multifamily acquisition candidates is to first narrow from region to Metropolitan Statistical Area (MSA).   From here, many people begin to segregate cities by quadrant (north, south, east and west). Wrong! Submarkets baby! It's all in the submarkets. From an article entitled "Submarkets Matter", to wit:

 ...between 40% and 50% of a property's overall performance is explained by sub–market factors while only 10% is explained by metropolitan factors (Submarkets Matter! Applying Market Information to Asset–Specific Decisions– Real Estate Finance).
 First identify submarkets (sections of a community) with positive attributes and then locate specific properties to acquire.   From "Mortgage Banking":

Comparing expected revenue growth over the next seven quarters with historical revenue growth over the past two years, one can identify those markets with either accelerating or decelerating rental growth rates. This is an important measure of market performance to the extent that the market "prices" apartment assets according to past, not expected performance. ("Scouting Top Apartment Markets", Mortgage Banking, – Geoff Rubin).

The above denotes "markets". I say applying the same map overlay to submarkets is where the rubber meets the road. From Co–star, http://costar.com :

Co–star Finds maps outlining specific, contiguous, non–overlapping geographic boundaries for similar commercial property types (eg, office, industrial, retail).

And once these contiguous, non–overlapping geographic boundaries of commercial properties are identified… then what? From my perspective, this is the starting line for acquiring quality multifamily assets.

A Telling Statistic

The home ownership rate is shrinking making for more apartment renters. Why? Higher family debt levels and tighter credit underwriting. According to a story by Reuters posted in the New York Times on October 8, 2010, the average American family has debt equal to 123% of disposable income. The Reuters articles goes on to say that at the current level of savings it will take four years for this number to come down to 100% of disposable income.

In 2010, American family debt is equal to 123% of disposable income

Thus, although the savings rate has increased in recent times, this savings is not being set aside for a home purchase, it is being utilized to decrease household debt. Therefore, considering home ownership now has higher cash requirements, the homeowner–to–be must first reduce household debt, then save for a down payment on a home.

What does this mean for multifamily owners? Consider, if we are four years away from American households "reducing" debt to 100% of disposable income, how many years after that will pass for individuals and families to meet cash down payment requirements for purchasing a home?

Fewer home owners means more renters

For apartment owners, the telling statistic is this: persistently high unemployment + high household debt + decreasing family income (down 8% from 2000–2009) equal fewer home owners as a percentage of the population. Fewer home owners means more renters.

This does not translate into immediate rent growth for multifamily apartment owners. There is still much dust to settle with respect to foreclosures, competition for renters from single family homes and family's sharing quarters based on economics (anything from junior staying home with Mom an extra year to four roommates sharing a two bedroom apartment).

Low multifamily construction starts, low interest rates
We have low multifamily construction starts to thank for absorption not falling off a cliff.   But that's no reason to get cocky. We also have a low interest rate environment to help multifamily owners get through this time– but for how long?

Knowing that the size of the renter pool is increasing does not reduce the need to be selective in tenant screening.   According to United Dominion (ticker UDR), a large multifamily REIT (Real Estate Investment Trust) a full one third of their tenant base resides with them for four years or longer.   This means they are very good at tenant selection.   Longevity of tenants equates to less turnover and lower turnover costs.

Multifamily property management and multifamily ownership remains a contact sport. Said in so many different ways; we proceed with caution. Yet with a long–term operational mindset.

5 Big, Easy Patterns

Since the turn of the century the U.S. population has grown almost ten percentage points. That's a lot of heads in beds! Recognizing a full one third of the population rents, how do we find these new customers for multifamily property owners? Where are all these new people? Let's find some clues in pattern recognition.

In this post we are excluding high–tech or big dollar data sources (like thematic mapping). We will discuss easy–to–find data points that provide guidance about demographics. This discussion relates directly to the acquisition of multifamily property and methods for gaining information about an acquisition candidate.

Consider this a due diligence starter kit for gathering market intelligence. Demographic data can tell us much about an area as we create layers of information related to a specific address– a specific acquisition target.

The following information sources are all public. There is little or nominal costs to obtaining information from these sources.

Big, Easy Patterns
Following are data sources that provide a "sense of place". Of course, for a place you've never heard of (or seen) this data alone is not sufficient for making investment decisions. However, these information layers will significantly enhance your location specific knowledge– including for places you *think* you know well.

#1. Census Data
The volume of information provided by United States Census Bureau can easily create that dear–in–the–headlights feeling. Start with the home page and go to **American Community Survey**. Go to: http://www.census.gov/acs/www/. This will provide "snapshot" data on any community without having to dive into the entire website. The Survey provides a starting point for obtaining demographic data for a certain place.

#2. Traffic patterns

The State DOT (Department of Transportation) can tell you where the traffic is… car traffic.

Metairie Louisiana is a place I lived for a year. Pre–Katrina (2005) Metairie was poised for growth. Significant retail development was underway and road construction was rolling including an expansion of interstates. I mean, they were loaded for bear.

So let's say we were to review the population data for New Orleans today, pre and post Katrina. The data will likely reflect some differentials (particularly at the census block group level). My guess is auto traffic has dropped off a cliff. Why is this important? Because tracing traffic volume and traffic patterns allows us to draw some conclusions and make predictions about future occurrences of growth based on this information.

When assessing a multifamily acquisition target, if the car count has dropped in recent years from, let's say, 9,000 cars a day to 3,000 cars per day; there is a reason. The "why" is the question. Large retail chains thrive on this data. Wall Street wants to know year–over–year "same store sales". Sales are based on traffic… foot traffic and car traffic. In this respect, there is a correlation between retail and multifamily.

#3. Building Permits

City/County Planning & Zoning. P&Z knows where builders are going to build…. even before builders do. They track not only all the paper related to building, but also utilities construction.

When a builder pulls a permit to build, they are committing real dollars to development and likely have already made an investment in excavation, Architectural and Engineering. They have also confirmed availability of water and electrical service. A builder pulling a permit intends to build.

Within a Census Tract, an over–lay of permits pulled and population growth can point an investor toward knowledge of construction trends and anticipated growth. No reason to buy in an area where builders have gone wild at the same time the population is shrinking. Stay away. Stay far away.

#4. Chamber of Commerce

The local Chamber has their hand on the pulse of the business community. It is there job to promote the community to the outside world. They know where development is occurring and who is shipping jobs into and out of the community.

Earlier this decade, in a very short period of time, there was a flood of apartment developments up for sale in Hazelwood, MO. A little digging found that the Ford Motor plant in that community was closing and with it thousands of jobs were leaving the area. Always check with the Chamber to see whose coming and whose going.

#5. FBI statistics

While this information can be daunting, it is important. It's also public information. For an area, focus on patterns of crime against people and property. What is the direction of the trend?

New York City in the 1980's had terrible crime. Yes, there is still crime there today, but not nearly to the extent as years ago. This single fact has enhanced not only the standard of living in the city, but has had a positive impact on property values.

Look at violent crime and rape. It's difficult to think about much less want to study. But wouldn't you prefer to know the trends prior to making a buying decision rather than after the fact?

Bonus! Here's the Best One

The Street Cop. These hard–working folks are your best source of on–the–ground information. They are honest reporters. Walk into the local precinct or Police station and ask to speak with the street cops that cover the area you have an interest in. If the officers are not available or too busy… come back later or make an appointment (remember: their shift and workload is not based your availability). The Police Officer's patrolling the very streets you have an interest in buying multifamily units know these streets.   Do not discount this.

Scratching the Surface

The preceding is a beginner's birds–eye view to a place. Professional demographic analysis is very expensive.

The methods presented here are not a substitute for professional reporting and market studies. The larger the investment, the more necessary professional market surveys become.

The preceding is not a substitute for a quality market study or in–depth due diligence. This post represents a starting point for accomplishing baseline demographic analysis.

Multifamily acquisitions is as much art as science. Yes, we have our hard numbers and stacks of financials. Yet at the end of the day we need people. People to rent, people to manage.

The financial data alone is a single slice of the picture representing the value of an asset. The greater determinant of real value is in understanding current and future utilization… and by whom. The "who" is identified by Demographic and Market Analysis!

Multifamily Demographics: Must Know Definitions

Prior to analyzing financials for a potential multifamily acquisition, there are two things we must know about a property; the what and the where. What type of property, in terms of quality, and where it is located. Without first distinguishing some characteristics about what and where there is no reason to devote time to a review of income and expenses. This post is about the where.

The Where – People
Markets are distinguished by size and quality (size does not always equate to quality, of course). When it comes to demographics the objective is to know as much as we can about the people that live in an area.

Using public information, we can identify a number of data points that assist in determining the relative financial strength of an area based on who lives there; such as average age, income and educational attainment. These three factors provide very good baseline information about a neighborhood or sub–market.

Block Group. Block Groups generally contain between 600 and 3,000 people, with an optimum size of 1,500 people. The census block is the smallest unit of geography for which Census 2000 data are tabulated.

Census Tract. A census tract is a small geographic area. The primary purpose of census tracts is to provide a nationwide set of geographic units that have stable boundaries. Census tract numbers are unique within a county. A census tract will have from 1,500 to 8,000 persons with the optimal number being 4,000 persons.

Metropolitan Statistical Area (MSA). Careful selection of MSA's can greatly decrease the probability of making an inferior investment. A metro area contains a core urban area of 50,000 or more population, and a micro area contains an urban core of at least 10,000 (but less than 50,000) population.

Each metro or micro area consists of one or more counties and includes the counties containing the core urban area, as well as any adjacent counties that have a high degree of social and economic integration (as measured by commuting to work) with the urban core (from www.census.gov/).

The Where – Markets and Cities

Primary Market. These are markets with over one million people in the MSA with all the amenities of a big city from airports (usually plural) to cultural access and cross–industry jobs. They are well defined, well known and have a cultural identity. These are big cities with big city sports teams, fourteen Olive Garden restaurants and multiple freeways and job centers. Examples: Philadelphia, Boston, New York, Chicago, Los Angeles.

Twenty–four Hour Cities. Primary markets with thriving down towns and never–say–sleep districts. Examples: New Orleans, Atlanta, Chicago, Miami, San Francisco. Note that 24–hour cities are often known by their name alone, even by just their airport code: SFO, MIA, and ATL.

Secondary Market. Secondary markets are smaller than primary markets but with similar synergy's sized to the population. They are usually self–sustaining, but without the expansiveness and do not possess the cultural heritage of primary cities. They may have a single professional sports team, or multiple farm teams. They will have a single primary commercial airport. Examples: Omaha, Nebraska, Birmingham, Alabama, Little Rock, AR, Oklahoma City, OK, Nashville, TN.

Tertiary Market. These markets may be in the sphere of influence of a primary or secondary market, but based on size and distance, they are…. tertiary. Many have small airports, but it is common for people to fly into the "larger" airport in a close –by city and drive to the tertiary locale. Examples: Waco, TX, Savannah, GA, Topeka, KS.

Frontier Market. These markets are further from primary and secondary cities than tertiary markets. Reviewing property in frontier markets requires local market expertise as they are often excluded from industry reporting data. These places are just "not on the map" from an institutional buyers perspective. They are the job center for their area, they possess solid community endeavors and will likely have a small commercial airport. Examples: Dubuque, IA, College Station, TX, Bloomington, IL.

The Style of Money

When it comes to multifamily demographics, including the level of household income and where people live, eagles do flock. Families with similar incomes tend to live in the same neighborhood. This includes high income families that choose multifamily. The style of money refers to amenities utilized by those with high incomes.

Starbucks now has over 17,000 stores. At one time, however, they were a small growing company. Where did they place their initial stores? In high income neighborhoods. Example: Identify any Ritz Carlton or Hyatt Regency hotel. You will find a Starbucks is within a stone's throw of each.

What are some of the amenities demanded by high income families? Easy right? Just start listing them. Good design. Security. Plush landscaping. Fitness facilities. Pet and laundry services. All good, but not enough.

People Buy Neighborhood

In multifamily, our customers are people buying many things; a place to live, proximity to employment and lifestyle. Put another way, they are buying interior space and exterior space, or access; access to a lifestyle defined by the style of money.

Is there really any difference between a nice scarf purchased at an airport kiosk and Saks Fifth Avenue? Yes. The difference is at Saks the purchaser obtains the scarf in a very nice Saks bag and carries said bag around for a while for other to see.

This feeling, this aura brings with it a certain standing, albeit brief. It is long enough, however, to create willingness for the purchaser to pay a premium.

The same applies to an address. One great example is the television show "Beverly Hills 90210". The number is nothing other than a zip code– but oh what a zip code. The median household income here is significantly higher than for other zip codes in Los Angeles. It is intriguing how this zip code can be utilized to market "adjacent" locations. It is common today to see for sale housing and for rent multifamily marketed as "90210 adjacent". The meaning being if you cannot live in this zip code, at least you can live next to it.

How often do you see a single luxury car dealer? Very seldom because they tend to be concentrated in one area (flocking again). When looking to buy multifamily income property, look beyond the asset in question to review competitive properties. Do they stand up to each other? Are they "competitively aligned"?

Often, multifamily properties need similar competitive properties to justify their pricing. In other words; competition is good. Competing against similar properties allows for an area to attract the same clientele. This remains true for attracting high income customers.

Case in point: find any McDonald's and there will be a Burger King not too far. The same applies for Apple–bees and Ruby Tuesdays. And again for Morton's Steakhouse and Ruth Chris… they flock together (yet again). See the pattern?

As a buyer of multifamily, segregating needs from wants and what tenants are willing to pay for in rent is more science than "feel". The subject really can be defined, reviewed and measured with high degrees of accuracy.

An initial focal point is knowing as much as possible about the customers and potential customers for the acquisition candidate under consideration. Demographics really do tell a story. Better yet, they can sometimes predict the future.

Mining Data and Finding Yield

Population is an aggregate number. Data mining within populations points us towards finding yield. Multifamily demographics are the study of populations within certain boundaries. Sometimes these boundaries are Metropolitan Statistical Areas (big cities), other times they are as small as a city block.

Finding yield begins with having a good multifamily product and is enhanced by knowing the motivations of your customers.

What we do in multifamily demographic analysis is break large pieces of information into smaller pieces of information specific to a place. Why? Because that's where the money is.

The study a "population" at the sub–market level is the very essence of the matter to understand underlying motivations that drive a particular group of people to live the lifestyle derived within the borders of a place. (Ah. Pausing to relish in the English language for a moment– back to reality).

More plainly: why is it that this group of people is willing to pay this amount of rent to live here? The ultimate "so what" question. What makes you so special (South Beach, Tribeca, Sunset Blvd) that people are willing to pay more to live at an address rather than at another similar address for less money?

Is it lifestyle, prestige, snobbishness, a sense of safety? One reason is self–imposed segregation. I am not referring to racial segregation, but economic segregation. People tend to live in neighborhoods with other people of similar economic strata. This transcends race, professions, religion and sometimes politics.

Information
A population is the total number of persons inhabiting a country, city, district or area. The body of inhabitants of a place. Knowing the population of a place represents a single data point that tells us very little. We learn if a place is big or small (relatively speaking). Looking at a trend–line of population speaks to the level of growth occurring over time.

What are the differentiating data points drawing a cohort with X income to a location? What motives our customers? What future occurrences will enhance or detract from a particular group living in a particular place? How do we survey to predict future outcomes in a place? These answers are found in demographics.

Knowledge

Demographics are the statistical characteristics of human populations (such as age or income) used especially to identify markets, or markets within markets (sub–markets).
Further definitions of demographics: the statistical data of a population, especially those showing average age, income, education. The characteristics of human populations and population segments, especially when used to identify consumer markets.

Insight

My definition of insight is gaining specialized knowledge from information. Determining the value of an asset lies within understanding the people who live in and around the subject property.

Without first having baseline demographic information there is no cause to "go see" a potential buy. Traveling to a property without first knowing the demographics, in my view, means all you are really doing is sight–seeing.

Real Estate as a Weapon

In war, real estate is the essential weapon. The high ground almost always wins. At least historically this was true in battles on the ground. From ancient times to the American civil war there are historic accounts of battles where those holding the strategic high ground won the day.

Looking at World War II, there are multiple examples of "buffer zones" between battlefields; area's that separated combat. Quiet zones that went un–touched even though war waged all around. One example being the French agreeing to surrender Paris in exchange for Germany not destroying the city via aerial and ground attack. Thus, Germany controlled France. The high ground was the capitol city.

When accessing real estate assets in present day terms, in many instances, you get a feel for a place by just being there. Like coffee houses, some are pleasant, warm and welcoming. Others can be just stand–offish and sterile. Others just make you feel un–easy. Without getting all touchy–feely, my point is that we all have intuition. When reviewing real estate assets for purchase or lease this is no time to ignore your gut.

I know, "gut checking" advice is difficult to add to the market analysis and catalogue under due diligence. This is why when reviewing assets we review the entire market area. Quiet and peaceful for one block in every direction excludes too many factors affecting a location.

Take Princeton, for Example. Princeton University has a master plan. Princeton is surrounded by many sub–par and privately owned dwellings. Here is quote from the Princeton Campus Plan 2016:

Princeton had to balance the needs and desires of two interdependent communities: the University; and the neighboring Princeton Borough and Princeton Township.

In this case, the big dog on campus is... the campus. How can a single small property owner interact with a historic, iconic University? Not very well, really. Other than to pray for fairness.

My point is as an owner or entity in acquisition mode it's important to know the surroundings of owned assets beyond what's on the next block or two. In densely populated cities two blocks may represent the entire market area including competitive assets. In tertiary markets competitive properties may be seven miles away (yet still in the employment corridor).

This is not to say that all competitors are enemies. Collaboration does come into play on occasion. But do not discount that in a micro–market real estate revenue can be a zero sum game. One where competitors will pay to have your signs torn down and the occasional window broken if only to make your asset look bad for a spell (we exclude here "real" crime such as arson and intimidation).

Competitors may click on your Internet pay–per–click advertising to drive your advertising cost up and send fake shopper tenants to take up staff time. Such tactics seem counter–intuitive to me, but these things happen all the time.

Be mindful of your assets in terms of their "place" in the market and their "place" in the community. In other words, do all you can to assure your real estate is not in use as a weapon, be it a buffer or shelter to those committing crimes. Cities and towns evolve all the time. Complacency is seldom affordable in the long term.

Gaining a sense of place requires a review of buildings, streets, "flow" and people.

Single–family Homes: For Sale, For Rent, Foreclosed

The home–ownership rate in the United States is decreasing. Therefore, more single–family will be utilized as rental. How is single–family housing impacting multifamily rental? So many homes are presently for sale, for rent or foreclosed it's hard to tell who's on first!

Bottom line is in 2011 with so many homes in various forms of "stasis" these homes are unavailable for rental– right now. Certainly, single–family rental is a direct competitor to multifamily rental. How big is this "shadow market" anyway?

According to the website Calculated Risk (www. calculatedriskblog.com) quoting from Census Bureau data, since 2004 there are 3.60 million homes built for sale that are being utilized as rental.

As the home –ownership shrinks from 68% to perhaps as low as 63% over the next few years single–family homes will become a larger percentage of the rental marketplace. With price differentiation, that's fine. With a multitude of owners each having a single rental that's trouble.

Landlords with a single rental seldom care about market rate rents. Their objective is to cover cost, to break–even or do a little better. The profit motive is secondary. Retaining the asset via rental is the objective.

Let's review the sources of single–family property rental inventory that will soon compete directly with multifamily.

For Sale Housing
According to Reuters, the average days on market of "for–sale" housing is over 900 days in New York (NY City excluded) and over 600 days in Florida.
Recent data from Trulia (www.trulia.com) has the average Days on Market in Phoenix as 48 days. After 48 Days on Market homes

in Phoenix, on average, are reduced in price by eight percent. Most notable is that 35% of for sale homes have had price cuts. Numbers are similar for Mesa, AZ, Minneapolis, MN and Long Beach, CA.

Most housing that is "for–sale" is not for rent. But presuming Days on Market continues to extend, this inventory will enter the rental market as in many instances the only other option for the home owner is foreclosure.

For Rent Housing

The number of single–family rentals cannot be ignored. In my view, in our current economy, this pending excess inventory represents several percentage points of occupancy that normally falls to multifamily. The number of for–sale homes turned into rentals will only grow as the home–ownership rate decreases. Whether because of economic uncertainty, the job market or reduced income, sentiment has changed towards home ownership.

For–rent single–family housing competes directly with multifamily, more so than ever as rental price points for single–family dips and as single–family owners attempt to generate cash flow by any means necessary to retain assets.

Foreclosed Housing

There are over four million homes in foreclosure or serious delinquency in the United States. According to Professor Wheaton of MIT single–family foreclosures are concentrated in four states. They are California, Arizona, Nevada and Florida.

Is this for–sale housing or something else? A short–sale is not for rent. Nor a home stuck in the legal system for months on end. Either way, it's housing unavailable for rental. For now...

Eventually, these markets will clear– all of them. Of the for–sale and foreclosed homes many will become rental. This will take years. Limited construction the last three years will assist in absorbing much of this inventory.

Consider, however, that as the home–ownership rate declines single–family will play a larger roll in the rental marketplace. Multifamily has a new competitor coming it's way with some volume. It's name is the single–family home.

Chapter 4

Financing

Financing the Deal with Seasoning

Trying to obtain multifamily acquisition financing today with 15% equity? Go to HUD or have a deal size twenty million dollars. For everyone else it's wait, look, and listen. Many lenders continue to be in hiding with "continued uncertainty" as their mantra. So how do you get a deal financed today? Look for seasoning– well seasoned mortgage bankers that know their stuff. No rookies. No "just graduated". Work with professionals.

Today's blog is not a discussion about due diligence and operator experience.   When searching for financing today there are no short–cuts. Loan–to–value (LTV) ratios are tighter than any time in the past ten years. Now, this is not necessarily a bad thing for a future healthy multifamily market. However, it is a big adjustment on all sides of the table (for lenders, buyers, sellers) as we all adjust to "normal" underwriting (i.e., doing deals that make sense to everyone, including lenders and operators and not just third–party fee earners).   We should all feel sorry for commercial appraisers today. How do they get their job done in this marketplace?

So where do you find the professionals? Who are they and where do they live? Usually, they are in your very own backyard. Whereas I'm dying to mention names here I'm going to take the high road and discuss a funnel approach for identifying people that know what they are doing.   But first let me state this: you have to be real. There is no value in chasing financing unless you as a borrower and the deal have legs (meaning the ability to stand). Everyone has been around the guy at the party that seems to like talking just to hear himself talk. Don't be that person.   If you have a deal and a reasonable opportunity to close on it then by all means go after it. If it's all hype save your breath and every one's time and move on to a deal you can do.

For deals under two million dollars a local lender is best; a local or regional bank.   Often this will extend to deals under $5,000,000.

They have average unit sales prices in their head. They know all the local third–party service providers. Once the loan amount exceeds $5,000,000 there is another world that opens in terms of financing. National and international banks, pension funds, private banks, funds and funds of funds, insurance companies and on and on. However, unless you have relationships established within one of these networks you will need "representation" to gain access. Meaning a <u>seasoned mortgage banker</u>. It's best to have a mortgage banker already on your team prior to an acquisition candidate in your sights.

Let's assume you know not one single solitary soul in the mortgage banking business. No one at all. Where do you find a banker? A <u>real</u> banker? Start with the **Mortgage Bankers Association** and focus on commercial bankers (<u>http://www.mortgagebankers.org/ default.htm</u>). Then identify those that work with your product type (multifamily) and those that have offices in your region of the country. Surf their websites and check out individual bankers. Look for one or two that have credentials (in terms of years of experience, experience in your product type and volume) and also to see if there are any "links" you can develop. Links include things that you and the banker may have in common. Perhaps you went to the same college or both worked for the same entity sometime back. An example is that their profile says they've closed $100 million dollars in loans in the last few years and their favorite team is the Orioles. Perhaps you have a rookie card from the best Oriole player ever. Call and brag! You understand my point. Find links and start a conversation.

Another place to look is within the National Association of Mortgage bankers <u>http://www.namb.org/</u>. If you want to see who is doing volume, peek at some deal structures at Crittenden <u>http:// crittendenonline.com</u> .

Keep networking. Find personal links. Identify deals that work and do your homework.

Multifamily Finance – A Borrower's Guide

By David Garfinkel

I first would like to offer kudos to Mr. Wilhoit on the formation presented in his blog on multi–family properties. Personally, I have enjoyed reading his insights, and his information on financing apartments is spot–on. Which leads me to the question; why does he need me to write an article on financing? I'm hopeful that you will find my insights as useful as his. My name is David Garfinkel and I am with NorthMarq Capital, a nationwide Real Estate Investment Banker/Mortgage Banker, based in St. Louis.

I'm going to start with Real Estate Finance 101, in 2010. Things have changed dramatically in the last 3 years. As a Real Estate Investment Banker, I typically source permanent, non–recourse financing. We represent Blue–Chip Life Insurance Companies, Wall–Street Conduits (at least when they were lending), and the GSE's (Freddie Mac and Fannie Mae). We also source HUD financing. And finally, we source Equity, Joint Ventures and Mezzanine Financing. When I say permanent loans, this can be short–term floating rate loans, 3, 5 or 7 year loans. But our typical bread and butter loan is a 10–year term and the interest rate is based on a spread over the 10–Year Treasury. HUD Financing can offer 35–40 year fixed rate loans, but that is a different animal.

The main sources of financing for a multi–family property are Freddie Mac and Fannie Mae, along with HUD and then Life Insurance Companies. Freddie and Fannie can lend up to 80% Loan–to–Value (or Loan–to–Purchase) on a non cash–out refinance. If a borrower is looking to pull out cash on a refinance, the LTV drops to 75%. A Life Insurance Company may be able to lend up to 75% LTV, even though that is not the benchmark it once was. HUD can lend up to 83.5% LTV on a non cash–out re–finance. Earlier I stated that our loans are non–recourse, and they typically are. However, the borrower/borrowing entity has taken on a much larger role in the analysis of a loan. Freddie/Fannie will now ask for a Personal Financial Statement up–front.

The Agencies want to know that they are dealing with a borrower that has the financial wherewithal to handle any issues that may arise at a property. They have also implemented minimum liquidity covenants (such as 10% of the loan amount, or 6–12 months of debt service if the loan gets large). My point is that borrower underwriting has become more restrictive, as has underwriting in general. Lenders will also ask for 3–years of historical information, as well as YTD and a current rent roll. Lenders will not look at a pro forma – they will only underwrite actual, in–place income. Lenders will also look at trends. For example, they will look at the Trailing 12 numbers, but also Trailing 6 and Trailing 3. If there is a declining trend, this can be problematic unless there is a good explanation. My point is that a loan gets much more analysis today than in the past. Good record keeping is essential.

On the flip side, long–term interest rates have almost never been this low. If you were locking rate today with Freddie Mac or Fannie Mae on an 80% loan, with a 10–year term, the interest rate would be approximately 4.50%. Fixed. For 10–years. If you were locking a HUD loan today, the all–in rate would also be approximately 4.50% Fixed. For 35–years (there are certain advantages/disadvantages of HUD that may affect your opinion on if this is the type of loan you want). For the right property, with the right borrower, in a good location, we will be able to find you an attractive loan in today's market.

This blog has contained different articles on running a property, maintaining a property, and buying a property correctly. All of these have an impact on the ultimate financing you will be able to obtain. And once you lock the interest rate for 10–years, this number becomes fixed and can greatly influence your cash–flow on a transaction. There are so many variables that can affect your profitability as an owner of multi–family properties. If you can lower your interest rate, the cash–flow increases. Sounds pretty simple. Well, it used to be, but don't get me wrong, there is capital available for multi–family properties.

I can be reached at dgarfinkel@northmarq.com with questions / comments.

Multifamily Financing: Finding Real Lenders

How do you tell the wheat from chaff when searching for multifamily financing? For starters, consider national names you know. When seeking multifamily financing the best of all worlds is to work with <u>someone you know</u> with a track record of getting multifamily loans closed.

The second best alternative in securing multifamily financing is a direct (first line) referral from <u>someone you know</u> that has closed a multifamily loan with the lender or correspondent. But what if you don't know anyone?

With no direct link to a mortgage banker, first; identify banks, lenders and correspondent lenders that have closed deals in your marketplace, on property's that is familiar to you– perhaps competitive properties.

Since mortgages are recorded in the public record, identify lenders closing multifamily loans in your marketplace. This is as easy as doing a public records search.

Next steps... no personal contacts, no loans closed in recent months? Cast a wider net and contact your extended network requesting introductions to lenders that have closed multifamily loans.

Still nothing? Start with correspondent mortgage bankers. They have established relationships with lines of communication to direct lenders, often pensions, life insurance companies and banks with large geographic footprints.

Who to stay away from:

- Companies asking for retainer fees in the first five minutes of the first phone call.
- Companies asking for retainer fees before knowing any of the salient deal points.
- Companies asking you to <u>send</u> retainer fees without ever asking to see financials on the deal.

There is nothing wrong with retainer fees. Many correspondent lenders require advance payment for third–party service providers (appraisal, environmental et al) along with the loan application and perhaps additional funds to secure your place in line in loan processing. In essence, it's a commitment fee that is a reflection of your seriousness in proceeding with the loan.

Real lenders are in the business of closing real loans. There are loans getting done today. The job of the Correspondent is to place loans that meet or exceed loan underwriting standards as set out by the company committing funds. Take the time to understand these standards prior to making application.

Do your homework. There is a small criminal element in every industry and ours is no exception. Protect yourself with knowledge, research and time…. taking the time to make further inquiries about those new to your circle. There is no replacement for time.

Thinking of Interest Rate Risk

With respect to long–term ownership of income property, the capital stack (including debt) should reflect ownership's objectives on preservation of capital, yield on invested capital and capital gains. Interest rate strategy is part of strategic planning in multifamily financing. Long–term mortgage financing should provide consideration for the entire term of ownership; from date of acquisition t0 disposition.

Since the Federal Reserve announced Quantitative Easing 2 (QE2) the five–year Treasury rate has only increased. There are so many inflection points in future interest rate sooth saying it makes for a mad world. The European Central Bank thinks inflation is an issue (in Europe). Mr. Bernanke believes the beast to be well under control (in the U.S.). Borrowers prefer low interest rates. Savers prefer higher interest rates. We are all very self–serving.

Inflationary Pressure Will Return

For the last five years we have become accustom to mortgage interest rates being relatively stable. Granted, underwriting standards have gone through a tornado and earthquake at the same time, but long–term interest rates have remained in a narrow band during this time. Note to self: this cannot continue forever. Inflationary pressure will return (see recent rises in food prices) and interest rates will again see double digits.

There is no method to predict when this will occur, however, we can plan forward utilizing debt as a stabilizing force. What does that mean? It means that ownership and their management teams cannot pretend to be surprised at large swings in interest rates.

Which Rates to Watch

Excluding times of hyper–inflation (seldom experienced in the U.S.) we are provided with notice of changes to the cost of money. Interest rates "trend" up and down. Watch the Fed Funds Rate and LIBOR (London Inter–bank Offer Rate). Keep an eye on the 5–year Treasury. Simple advice, yes, but consider this as an integral part of protecting the value of a multifamily portfolio.

Consider that a one percentage point increase in interest rates equates to $7,500+ per million dollars borrowed– per year. Multiply this for a $100 million dollar portfolio and the impact is exponential! It can really move the break–even point.

Conventional wisdom is that having long–term fixed rates loans on income property solves interest rate exposure. Not true. Try finding a commercial mortgage fixed for thirty years. This is a rare find today. Whereas amortization may be for thirty years, the term of the fixed interest rate will be 3, 5 or 10 years.

Stagger Mortgage Maturity Dates

There is nothing wrong with variable rate mortgages. They have their place in a well–positioned portfolio. They only become dangerous when over–utilized, when they represent a substantial portion of debt for a single owner/operator. One simple method of spreading interest rate risks is to stagger maturity dates.

Preservation of capital is home base. It is the cornerstone of wealth. Paying attention to interest rates and their impact on cash flow and value is part of protecting home base.

Multifamily Financing: CMBS 2.0

By David Garfinkel

Welcome to multifamily financing in the 21st century. It's a brave new world! CMBS 2.0 is here as 25 shops have recently set up for Commercial Mortgage Backed Securities (CMBS) lending. The forecast is for $40–$60 Billion of CMBS loans this year.

It is time to start thinking again about Life Insurance Companies and CMBS 2.0. In 2007, CMBS loans exceeded $225 Billion Dollars. This dipped to $3 Billion in 2009. That is a huge amount of capital that left the lending market and was part of the multifamily financing challenge over the last few years.

This is the second guest article I have written for Multifamily Insight, and again I offer my kudos to this blog. The vast articles are interesting and insightful. My first article was titled "Multifamily Financing: A Borrowers Guide" and it addressed the challenges and pitfalls of obtaining a commercial loan in today's market.

I focused on the three main lending sources of multifamily loans; Freddie Mac, Fannie Mae and HUD. These three sources are collectively doing 90% of all multifamily loans today. Another theme was that borrower underwriting has become more challenging and diligent. And as always, good record keeping is essential.

Banks were not lending, and Life Insurance Companies could pick and choose what loans they funded (and remember, many Life Companies have maturing loans every year that is part of their overall funding program). If there is $50 Billion of CMBS loans funded in 2011, this will bring more capital into the market place, and hopefully ease some pressure.

CMBS loans underwritten in 2007 will be very different from a CMBS loan underwritten today, and this is a good thing. Gone are the days of the 10–year interest–only loans, underwriting pro forma rents and a lender waiving reserves, escrows, etc (except in the case for low leverage loans). The CMBS loan of 2011 (now referenced as CMBS 2.0) will be underwritten diligently, the way it was intended when CMBS was first introduced.

Maximum Loan–to–value is currently 75%, while some CMBS shops are sticking to 70% LTV. Now, I won't be surprised if this eventually pushes back up to 80%, but I don't see this happening in the near future. I think everyone is waiting to see how many loans can get done by CMBS and how the paper sells.

There is less negotiation in the loan document process, as CMBS shops need to paper the transaction appropriately to make sure it sells. Borrowers will still have challenges talking to a loan servicer or getting a friendly voice on the phone should issues arise. But the fact that 25 firms have set up shop is good news – I guess we'll see if they all can survive, but this is still positive news for borrowers.

A more borrower friendly source of capital is Life Insurance Companies. NorthMarq has relationships with over 50 Blue–Chip Life Insurance Companies. Life Companies were the major source of capital in 2008 and 2009, but they still didn't win many multifamily loans due to the competitiveness of Freddie Mac, Fannie Mae and HUD.

Today, they are actively competing with Freddie and Fannie and are getting their share of multi–family loans. Don't get me wrong, CMBS lenders and Life Insurance Companies will still underwrite and scrutinize a loan, and they will still analyze borrower strength, the market, the competitive set and do everything that a smart lender should do. But CMBS and Life Companies are opening up the lending landscape not only on multifamily loans, but other income producing properties.

Finally, Freddie Mac, Fannie Mae and HUD are also still lending, so there are more options for loan opportunities. All of this is good news for potential borrowers. Yes, there are still problem loans. Yes, lenders are still foreclosing on assets. But for the right borrower, with the right property, with good stable history, there are loans to be had again in 2011.

 I welcome any questions or comments, or any questions about market conditions and interest rates. I can be reached at dgarfinkel@northmarq.com.

Banks, Litigation and Mortgages

What a mess– one big mess. Reports say major banks may
have sold more than $200 Billion dollars in fraudulent mortgage
securities. Large banks will be in litigation for years to come from
the recent implosion of mortgage–backed securities. At the end of
the day, who wins?

JP Morgan and Bank of America are on the hit list. Big targets
all. I'm not taking sides here. My concern is for the American
banking system. Sub–prime mortgages were never a bad thing.
Packaging sub–prime mortgages and selling them as AAA credit
was the terrible thing. And rating agency have no blame???
Law suits by investors, State Attorney Generals and big brother
himself are all getting in on the action. Goldman Sachs is out of
the mortgage–back securities business altogether.

Question: if banks diverting billions of dollars (with a B) to
address litigation, what happens to their ability to lend? You
remember lending, the primary business of banking? If this
litigation were a bell curve, we are at the starting gate of the curve
at 0.01/0.01.

No matter the resources of an entity at some point they reach a
point of saturation, or exhaustion. This action, years upon years
of litigation, will redirect human and monetary resources of major
banks away from their primary business mission– lending. In
other words: they will have fewer people and fewer dollars to lend
to real businesses and real people.

Today, that may not seem like a big deal as demand for loans is
below dirt anyway (beyond stuck in the mud). The credit crisis as
noted the day after the Lehman bankruptcy in 2008, showed many
a crack in the system; one being that businesses being cut off from
access to credit do strange things– like not pay their people. And
the ripple, once started is impossible to retract.
I believe in capitalism. I believe in competition. I also believe
generational litigation will directly impact GDP as HUGE amounts

of human capital will be deployed to address these potential wrongs. I just don't see a winner or one new loan generated from all this. Sad.

http://www.bloomberg.com/news/2011–09–22/bank–of–america–filing–fee–case–may–open–new–front–in–mortgage–lawsuits.html

Real Estate Finance and Demographic Trends

With pent up demand for multifamily why is the construction pipeline slow to respond? Credit underwriting. With a plethora of real estate assets available for sale why is sales volume year–over–year about the same? Credit underwriting. Real estate finance is not for the faint of heart. The credit pipes frozen in 2008 continue to un–thaw three years later. And reading demographic trend tea leaves is becoming a tricky business.

With no end in sight to the current credit crisis, multifamily construction is hampered to the Nth degree. Multifamily owners benefit now, yes, with less product in the pipeline and pressure on rents. However, the need persist for more multifamily housing even as economy begs for construction jobs. With the lingering glut of foreclosures and limited consumer demand for new homes, housing starts have few friends.

"Since the beginning of this recession the home ownership rate in the United States has dropped from 69% to 66%" – RBC Capital Markets

In the not–to–distant–future, real people will need real multifamily starts as a housing shortage develops. We require a higher level of housing starts to support population growth– multifamily housing starts. Recent quarterly data reflects a "spike" in construction starts, yet they are well below historic norms and significantly below the level necessary to maintain pace with demographic trends. But is this true?

Yes it is true that our economy can benefit from increases in multifamily construction. So do we really need the housing starts going forward? Is there a pending housing shortage? Here are some facts:

- Fact: U.S. population growth is slowing to around one percent
- Fact: The average age is increasing to over 35 years old
- Fact: The U.S. birthrate is slowing

Makes you think, yes? Commercial lenders ponder these same conditions. Commercial Mortgage Backed Securities (CMBS) has had resurgence this year, but at levels that pale by comparison to previous years. They say to themselves "what's the hurry?" Not only do we have a current glut of single–family housing, we can see slowing population increases and other headwinds. Thus, in underwriting they are taking their sweet time assuring to cross every T when it comes to approving new loans including those with higher risks quotients– like construction loans.

I continue to believe we will experience a housing shortage, or at the very least, a squeeze by 2015. A diminishing housing stock (losses from flood, fire and demolition) dove–tailing with such low current levels of new construction will lead to double–digit rent growth again for an extended period.

Looking towards 2020 and 2030 I do see a creep from the facts noted earlier in terms of lower need. As people age, they generally need less space. The wild hair here is in–migration. Twenty years from now will America still be the place "go to" place for those with an entrepreneurial spirit and free market mentality? I hope so.

So before heaping more coals on the head of y0ur mortgage banker based on their slowness to respond, consider they are reviewing these same demographic dynamics as to when housing stock will balance with need. Even with with massive computing power and more than just a few well paid mathematicians the answer remains elusive.

Chapter 5

Opinion

Your Home is Not a Real Estate Investment

My house is not real estate? Well, yes, it is "real estate". It's just not a real estate "investment". Real estate investing represents an on–going part of a well diversified investment strategy. Most investors are under–allocated in real estate believing that their personal residence is part of this allocation. Excluding your home, do you own real estate? Your home, while looking like real estate, is not a real estate investment you look to for yield or income.

Investment real estate provides four different forms of yield. They are:

- Income – as derived from rents or other ancillary income generated

- Tax shelter – provided by depreciation of the physical asset over time

- Appreciation – the increase in value over time

- Mortgage pay down – the increase in value created as income is utilized to decrease debt

Allocation theory suggests that a portfolio should have between 5% and 15% of assets in real estate (excluding your personal residence). Thus, investors should have between $50,000 and $150,000 in real estate for every one million dollars in net worth.

When excluding your personal residence, what percentage of your investment portfolio is in real estate? Direct real estate ownership provides a buffer to the daily market swings in stocks and bonds. Real estate is an important part of a balanced portfolio.

The Three P's of Multifamily: People, Property and Paper

Every successful owner of multifamily property must deal with the Three P's of real estate in a proactive manner. They are; people, property and paper. Following are examples that fit into each category. This is by no means an all–inclusive list, just a sample of items that impact the value of your property.

People. Every business is built on relationships and the multifamily business is no different.

- Customer contact – Who is the public representative of your property? Who is the first person they meet when considering your property as their residence? Are they representing you well? I remember reading about the CEO of Avis having an eye–opening experience when calling his own company to rent a car. Not all was well on the home front.

- Maintenance. Is maintenance not only responsive but respectful? There is more to customer service that just fixing the issue. Along with promptness, courtesy always goes a long way.

- Vendors. Can you call a plumber at 5:01 PM and not get hit up with an after hour charge? What is your relationship with vendors? Take the time to get to know when their slow season is and hire them during those times. This will go a long way to get you closer to the top of the list when you need a good turn.

- Banking. This industry has changed dramatically in recent times but do not discount the need to have a working relationship with you bank. Do you have a "go to" person for not just loans but everyday banking services? Is there more than one person at the main branch that knows your name?

Property. What is the first impression and lasting impression your property presents to current and future customers?

- Management. Are your management systems in place and being followed?
- No unit is ready for showing until its ready. No shortcuts here. You only get one chance to make a first impression.
- Is landscaping in good order and trash picked.
- If the pool is open is must be sparkling and be ready for use.

Paper. Paper represents the documents that secure your ownership position. Without it, there is no "paper trail" to prove to anyone your right to the income stream created by the asset.

- Ownership documentation.
- Ownership structure.
- Financing. Bank loans and other financing documents.
- Insurance. Is your insurance in order and up to date? Do you have emergency phone numbers for weekend emergencies? Hail and wind damage does not wait until Monday to be addressed. Does your manager have a camera on hand to take immediate photos of an occurrence?

When the Value of Money is Zero

What can multifamily property owners do when the value of money is zero? Finding investment yield in today's marketplace is a challenge. Options are limited on a risk–adjusted basis. Seeing advertisements for CD's yielding 2% is not exactly inspiring investors. Even municipal bonds seem to have more risk as rating agencies have become suspect. Property owners have an alternative to seeking yield from these sources.

Paying down existing debt is sometimes a good alternative to keeping cash. For example: if the mortgage on your apartment portfolio has a 6% interest rate and your savings account is paying 1% then there is sound logic to paying down the mortgage versus keeping cash. To a point, of course. This does not apply to reserve cash and/or operating funds.

One thing you may have noticed as a multifamily property owner in the last eighteen months is that even though valuations have fluctuated greatly rent rates have remained steady. This bodes well for future value as population increases meet the mean streets of decreased housing (and multifamily) starts.

Consider additional debt reduction from the perspective of a dollar cost averaging strategy like for any other investment. Mortgage reduction is not the place to invest your last dollar or rainy day reserves, but if you believe that the market is cyclical (as I do) then this is a solid alternative investment to non–yielding treasuries or non–dividend paying stock.

It's necessary to believe in the property markets long–term to consider making such an investment in owned assets. My perspective is to buy long. The investment cycle we are in at present is archaic to say the least. While deflation could occur I believe the probability is remote. And whereas inflation can be a property owner's friend, I would not rely on this aspect of the economic cycle in the next few years.

So before considering buying into that oil and gas well (when you have NO experience in that industry) or purchasing civil war currency (that your best friend loves to collect) consider additional mortgage pay down on owned assets (revenue producing owned assets).

Always keep cash reserves. The recommendation posed here is for dollars looking for a yield.

The Impact of Declining Sales in Single Family Homes

How does the sale of single–family homes influence the multifamily marketplace? From this week's Washington Post there is story on the declining number of sales of existing homes written by Dina Elboghdady and Ariana Eunjung Cha. The headline reads:

Sales of existing homes plunge to 15–year–low

The report notes there is a 12.5 months' supply of homes on the market whereby the norm is six months. Is this good or bad for multifamily owners? What impact does this have on "for rent" apartments? Here are my thoughts.

For many the non–sale of their existing residence places life on hold. Being unable to sell their primary residence and relocate stops many from making any other major life decisions, such as accepting job transfers or looking for work in other cities.

Ours is a transient society– we like our freedoms. One of these is the ability to move about the country at will. Job mobility is common, but less so when the real estate market is not clearing sales at a steady pace. If accepting a job is predicated on having to sell the primary residence this creates increased financial stress to say the least. More so when looking at a one year supply of "for sale" homes.

Prior to the recession, some communities (usually in the Sunbelt) would see as much as a 50% turnover in home sales in a five year period. Little Bobby and Mary, if they stayed in the same school system, would graduate high school with perhaps two of ten people with whom they started first grade.

Home ownership, historically, is right around 67% of the U.S. population. Meaning, 33% of the population rents. During the last few years the home ownership rate skyrocketed to over 70%. We are well aware of the causes from no–doc mortgage loans to ultra–safe (said in jest) securities packaging of mortgages to yield–hungry investors.

In theory, as the historic home ownership rate comes back down to normal this should mean more renters entering the marketplace bringing balance back to the aforementioned 67% and 33% mix of owners to renters.

A confused mind always says no
I contend based on the extended nature of the recession this "balance" will indeed take some time to return as there is a broad mix of housing still in flux. This includes a myriad of mortgage litigation, foreclosures, short sales, the non–dissolution of Fannie Mae and Freddie Mac. All of these matters assist in maintaining indecision on the part of buyers and sellers. Thus, for as long as people are un–sure of what is going to happen next, they will to the best of their ability…. Do nothing.

Pouring Jell–O from a Pitcher into a Small Glass
We have even created new terms to describe the fractured marketplace. These terms include "negative equity" and "constructive destruction" (when an old house or partially–built new house is torn down thus reducing housing inventory).
The continued stubborn employment reports also provide cause to pause in terms of making long–term home buying decisions. This all weighs on the "for sale" housing market which impacts the rental market.

So what's happening to the rental market?
Here are a few of the positives and negatives occurring in the rental market based on the continued "stasis" in home ownership.

Positives
- Reduction in home ownership means more people in the renter pool. Some will purchase a smaller or less expensive home, some will rent.
- A larger renter pool, in markets with job stability, should add a firmer bottom to rental rates assisting in burning off concessions faster. This doesn't mean a rapid rise in rent growth, however.

175

Negatives

- As noted earlier, a confused mind often says no– to everything. There are some that will remain in their home to the bitter end– even past foreclosure. They are neither home owners nor renters. This represents more people than one might think.
- Former home owners become one half of a future rental. Whether single or married, with or without kids, many people "double up" into rental housing. Or, move in with a friend and help to pay their mortgage. Either way, this survival tactic, while admirable, continues as the state of flux in the economy remains.

I contend the underlying lag in home sales along with the shadow rental market (for sale homes that are being rented) continues to impede the rental market. The saving grace for apartment owners is that construction starts of new multifamily are at historic lows so multifamily inventory is growing at a snail's pace.

Without rent growth, operations require extra scrubbing to increase NOI. And that's the best way to operate today. Keep pace with peer property's and make sure yours is up to speed to the best of your financial ability. This should keep good operators operating until our economy picks up some steam.

The Moral Hazard of Housing

The multifamily business is a lot like most men, simple. Home ownership would seem to be a simple thing also, but it is not. Jerry Seinfeld wonders out loud how any man can attract any woman, we men, being as simple as we are. Even so, women keep falling for us. So while no man is deserving, women are attracted to men, even with all our faults. Kind of like mortgage companies and consumers over the last decade. Mortgage companies love the mortgage consumer. Simple as we were….

Queue: Enter Mortgage Banking Giants

In "get–a–mega–mortgage–for–nothing–land" everyday consumers were being courted by all manner of companies asking them to sign on for a new mortgage. Who doesn't like being courted? Families that thought an older tract house was their best living could now afford a new 3+3+3 (three bedroom, three bath, three car garage). Did I mention it was a new house! Multitudes that had never dreamed of home–ownership were now home owners. With introductory mortgage rates the sky was the limit.

Since, the house of cards has fallen. While mortgage rates remain low, the context of these vast home–ownership purchases has changed dramatically with significant decreases in home valuations to go along with stock market losses and high unemployment.

Fast–forward to October, 2010. Foreclosures across the country were momentarily" on hold" as the new systems brought into service by the mortgage giants are found to be void of actual mortgage documents. You know, things like recorded deeds and notes with original signatures. Silly judges are actually asking to see the originating documents. "How rude is that" says the mortgage servicer with only electronic numbers to convey in court. JP Morgan Chase has announced a set–aside of one billion dollars to "address" the foreclosure issue.

The Seduction was Real

Washington Mutual was a mammoth of a company (WAMU).

So was Countrywide. WAMU imploded in the sub–prime crisis. Countrywide, which at one time had a market cap of $20 Billion dollars, was sold to Bank of America for $4 Billion dollars. Before the crash, these companies fought over consumers with mortgage rates and terms never before seen in history. New acronyms were created just to express the vast magnitude of mortgage products available. A famous story from WAMU underwriting was about a man that claimed to earn a six figure income as a Mariachi singer. Since this was a "no–doc" loan the only confirmation of income was a photo in the file with the man in his costume.

The Blame Game

Mortgage servicers tell consumers all day long that it is their obligation to pay the mortgage debt as described. Consumers balk at continuing to pay for a mortgage on a home with a valuation less than the mortgage amount. Lots of finger pointing. Lots of law suits. Lots of tears. I tip the majority of blame to the side of the mortgage professionals many of whom knew from day one of underwriting that default rates on certain loans types were going to be through the roof.

I'm not referring to retail mortgage brokers. I'm referring to the upper–tier offices of major companies running billions of dollars. Those with ultra–sophisticated super–computers running algorithms on default losses. Those with the ability to determine just how fast they needed to re–package and re–sell loans in the CMBS market before default rates hit claw–back provisions.

In this circle, the Jester is the rating agencies going along for the ride with the rest of the court. The gauntlet is set against the serfs... It's an intellectual battle between an Ivy League educated lawyer and an 18 year–old who dropped out of school in 8th grade. Joe Public doesn't stand a chance.

Part of the American dream is home ownership. Even so, some blame must remain with consumers who knew in their heart of hearts that the mortgage deals being offered were not sustainable. It is certain the Puritan ethic was overtaken by lust of the flesh – at full speed.

Viewed from a purely financial perspective many should walk away from their mortgage.   But this is not just a financial decision, as walking away means also leaving one's home and the stature that comes with being a home owner.   Further, it's embarrassing. And who really wants to leave their familiar surroundings? Particularly based on the premise of a system–wide meltdown? We all bleed red. And as has always been true, the lowest man on the totem pole hits the ground first.

So, as women will always love (simple) men, mega–mortgage companies will always love (simple) consumers.

Things We Know

Following are some thoughts we are certain will impact the multifamily business in 2011– regardless of the changing tides in politics. When it comes to mass media, "We the People" are often left with limited factual data of stature, less so with respect to multifamily data points that affect our business.

As the saying goes "all politics is local". So it is with apartment management. While it's nice to know the national trends, the day–to–day battle is local. Here, it is my intent to note national data points that will influence every local property owner. They are inescapable facts that I leave to your own interpretation.

As I've mentioned in this space before, I really like Bloomberg Radio. There's no better place to obtain a broad–brush of all things economic in terms of opinion, trends and conjecture.

While so much of the media attempts to think for us, Bloomberg, in my opinion, provides independent thought with a depth of detail allowing an observer to draw their own conclusions. In a single hour, the amount of factual data can be so overwhelming as to leave listeners with a yearning to sip an entire bottle of wine while in deep contemplation. Granted, one must be selective on the hour to obtain this depth of gestalt–level cognitive interruption.

So much for waxing poetic. Each fact presented here impacts our national economy and your local property and the property management business. The facts:

Fact: It's Wednesday morning, President Obama is…. President. Regardless of your political stripes, this administration has two (or more) years to shape policy.

Fact: QE2 is here (Quantitative Easing by the Federal Reserve). This fact, along with other measures taken by the Fed, will keep interest rates low for the next several quarters– or longer.

Fact: As the money supply expands, Quantitative Easing will dislodge any sense of potential deflation. An increase in the money supply often leads to greater inflationary pressure. Prices rise, if for no other reason, because more dollars are chasing the same amount of goods. An increasing money supply also reduces the value of debt instruments.

Fact: Unemployment will remain high through 2011. Even with a steady increase in job creation, unemployment will remain above eight percent (8%) through next year.

Fact: The U.S. population is growing "concurrent" with housing starts well below a level necessary to keep pace with the rising population. This fact could create a housing shortage as early as 2014. However, unless job growth really kicks in big time, the more likely conclusion is that we will see average household size increase.

Housing and Health Care

The economics of multifamily housing is something I understand. The economics of health care is a complete mystery to me. I believe the two have a strong correlation going forward.

Apartment rents are a component/percentage of household income. So is medical care. As costs of discretionary items increase as a percentage of income (things like health care), the location of housing will become more of a focal point.

Multifamily housing close to job centers and transportation hubs is usually more expensive than apartments at further distances from these points. Well, that's fair; multifamily housing that is closer to jobs requires less money for transportation. Easy trade–off. Easy to understand. There is no such trade when it comes to health care.

According to the Depart of Labor, in 2007 housing represented 32% of consumer discretionary income. Health care represented 28%

Can that be true? The two things necessary to sustain life are food and shelter. How is it a single discretionary item could possibly be such a big percentage of income???

The American middle class has more to consider however. Consider these facts:

- Many states tax food. Food costs continue to rise often as a function of fuel costs and speculation (did you know both Coke and Pepsi buy corn futures because their products no longer use sugar– they use corn syrup).

- Transportation to our place of work is a necessity. No transportation, no work. We cannot drive a car without state–mandated "must have" auto insurance.

Recently we've been in a zero percent inflation environment. This doesn't seem to slow the increase in health care costs, however. Here is where I see housing and health care colliding:

Increases in health care costs continue to Erode Disposable Income

With medical expenditures taking up a greater percentage of disposable income, this leaves less income for housing.   Certainly, we could say the same thing for food, fuel costs or utilities as all impact disposable income.

But health care is the one item where it comes down to your money or your life in some instances. Moving to a less expensive location does nothing to impact this cost. From the Los Angeles Times on January 5, 2011:

Another big California health insurer has stunned individual policyholders with huge rate increases — this time its Blue Shield of California seeking cumulative hikes of as much as 59% for tens of thousands of customers March 1. Blue Shield's action comes less than a year after Anthem Blue Cross tried and failed to raise rates as much as 39% for about 700,000 California customers. By Duke Helfand, Los Angeles Times

Even though the cost of housing (shelter) has remained stable or decreased in recent years, somehow health care costs increases year after year. Why?

One objective of health care reform is to bring health care to a greater percentage of the population.   This is a good thing. Politics aside, my belief is care should not be denied to anyone in need. As a Capitalist, however, I recognize we must determine a methodology to pay for said care.   Here is another way of saying Health Care will impact housing:

With greater access to medical care Life Spans will increase

Again, another pending collision between health care and housing….. Where are all these people going to live? Where are we on the development path of seniors care versus day care?

Is the residential housing complex (owners, operators and builders) prepared to convert student housing to assist living as demographics dictate changes? (Sidebar: In some states prison construction is greater than school construction– a damning reflection on our society).

Now that we are living longer concurrent with spending a greater percentage of our income on medical care– what's the end game? It seems the list of "necessities" gets only longer starting with food and shelter–and some would add cell phone service. The <u>real</u> short list: Food, shelter, utilities, medical, transportation.

I have questions. Yes, our standard of living is better than previous generations. But at what costs? Note the cost of housing is correlated to household income. Many households have two incomes. Is this now a mandated necessity to maintain housing affordability for a middle class standard of living?

One suggestion to remedy spirally medical costs is proffered by Clayton Christensen (<u>http://www.claytonchristensen.com/</u>) author of the book Disrupting Class.

Doctor Christensen suggests that the high costs of medical care as provided by high costs environments (like hospitals) should not be torn down. Instead, the provision of medical services should expand to lower costs environments, like clinics and in–home treatment through the utilization of technology.

Calling all social science graduate students (and Masters Students in Real Estate) for further study.......

The Meaning of a Weak Dollar

What impact does a weak dollar have on the U.S. multifamily market? For starters, a weak dollar brings added foreign equity capital to the asset class in the United States. Multifamily property is an established, known investment.

Apartments are a very stable investment. For multifamily buyers, when price decreases for reasons unrelated to operations of the underlying asset, this usually signals a buying opportunity. This is what occurs when the value of the U.S. dollar decreases versus other currencies.

Here is the definition of a weak dollar from www.Investorwords. com:

Dollar that can be exchanged for only a small or decreasing amount of foreign currency. A weak dollar means that the U.S. dollar cannot buy very much of another currency... A weak dollar usually lends to high exports and low imports, the opposite of a strong dollar.

In the broadest definition, a weak dollar means U.S. goods are less expensive for foreign buyers. This includes apartments. In other words, when the dollar is weak, foreign buyers can buy more U.S. apartment property with their currency.

While currency's bounce daily, property values, are cyclical. Multifamily property values do fluctuate, but not daily. And while multifamily assets are illiquid, they are stable, long–term investments– a safe haven.

For investors searching for yield, multifamily assets provide a steady and predictable income stream. For proof, note that every pension fund of size has significant real estate holdings– from 5% to 15% of total holdings.

Recently, the U.S. dollar hit an all time low against the Japanese Yen. Last year, around the time of the Greek debt crisis, the Euro dropped from $1.48 to $1.29. Currencies are a bouncing ball best left to those that trade– daily. There is no such thing as a "passive" currency trader.

There are thousands of passive multifamily real estate investors, however. From investors in Real Estate Investment Trust (REIT"s) to local owners that have a small share in a Limited Liability Company (LLC) that owns apartment units.

To a currency trader direct ownership of multifamily assets seems like a slow–moving business. After all, currency traders can execute a buy trade in nanoseconds whereas it can take three to six months to close on a single apartment property. Currency traders can sell with the click of a mouse whereas an apartment building can take six months to two years to sell.

Weakness in the dollar (even cyclically) will continue to bring foreign investors into the multifamily asset class in the United States. For all the talk of China becoming a rising economic power, the United States economy continues to dominate world trade, world politics and militarily. And with that dominance comes the power of a having the world's reserve currency.

My view is that multifamily assets represent a cornerstone investment; an investment class kept in the family generation after generation. I say buy apartments in dollars.

Core Inflation Expectations and Rent Growth

It is no secret food and fuel prices are increasing. We see it in every trip to the grocer or gas station. The market basket of items utilized to determine the "official" inflation rate is a moving target. How do we tie multifamily rent growth to inflation? The answer is we do not.

We do not tie rent growth to such a broad number as core inflation expectations. This number is a barometer of expectations. Multifamily rent growth is a function of dynamics occurring in the market where a property operates. Granted, inflationary pressures occur based on input costs associated with operations. This is industry specific inflationary inputs and has little to do with global commodity variances.

What is core inflation?

A definition from Investopedia: Core inflation is a measure of inflation that excludes certain items that face volatile price movements. Core inflation eliminates products that can have temporary price shocks because these shocks can diverge from the overall trend of inflation and give a false measure of inflation.

A further explanation of core inflation from Investopedia: Core inflation is most often calculated by taking the Consumer Price Index (CPI) and excluding certain items from the index, usually energy and food products. Other methods of calculation include the outlier's method, which removes the products that have had the largest price changes. Core inflation is thought to be an indicator of underlying long–term inflation.

For multifamily property managers and owners, I believe core inflation expectations represent just one metric for measuring projected rent growth; it is not the be–all–end–all number to watch. I know owners that tie annual rental increases to the rate of increase in social security benefits– regardless of market dynamics. This is not a reasonable or sustainable rent growth strategy.

Commentators project inflation is "X" percent excluding....
auto and aircraft OR excluding food and commodities OR
excluding fuel and natural gas. Can anyone just tell us the real
inflation number– please~! According to macro–economist the
reason for excluding items with "price shocks" is because they
are "transitory". Certainly, it does not seem that way when it
cost $80 for a tank of gas.

Market Dynamics Drives Rent Growth

More than any other factor it is market dynamics that drives
multifamily rent growth; the competitiveness of your asset as
compared to other assets in the cohort. And price is not the sole
dynamic. We compete against other multifamily property in
the submarket. Property does not compete against core inflation
expectations.

Livability, safety, access to job centers, responsiveness, positive
management control, energy efficiency, landscaping.... most
of these are not directly correlated to price so much as property
management and ownership philosophy.   I am not suggesting
inflation expectations is an absolute non–factor in pricing rent
growth, however, it is ancillary to head–to–head competition at the
property level.

Property managers must consider year–over–year revenue
gains accounting for vacancy, concessions and other detractors
from revenue. Multifamily property managers cannot rely
on inflationary gains to rescue revenue growth. They must
manage with long–term objectives in mind irrespective of price
movements in corn, copper or gold.

Day Trading Versus Real Estate Investing

Why am I writing about day trading when my profession is multifamily real estate? Because many of the same mistakes occur in both professions.

Minute by minute investing is a part of daily life now for many people (sometimes by the nano–second). Day trading for John Q Public started several years ago with the advent of the internet. It became so prevalent that even Charles Schwab had offices converted to use by day traders. I profess to know nothing about day trading other than it seems very dangerous for any novice.

It is in the same category as hawking "nothing down" real estate to the masses. Sure, it can be done, but how does a person that makes widgets by day measure the risk of investing in real estate by night, as a hobby? Do they know their entire net worth could be at risk by not adhering to the "special" instructions on page 232 of Guru's #21215"s playbook?

Notice that almost anytime the federal government attempts to do something quickly the results are perilous. I am excluding examples here to avoid politicizing the question except to say whether its war or distribution of vaccines, we probably want our government to act assuredly, not quickly.

The same holds true for investing in multifamily real estate. As a full–time professional, there are "deals" that come to my attention every day. One or two, in the course of a year, requires fast action.

I have nothing against day traders. A select few know their business because it is their business. A recent commercial on Bloomberg Radio is about how a man loses his job and says it's the best thing that ever happened to him. Why? Because now he's a day trader! Right. And I teach ballet on weekends.

Whether multifamily real estate or day trading, take the necessary time to learn the craft. One hundred hours of training will save you one thousand hours of heartache.

The American Economy in 2012

Most government stimulus packages end this year. As of mid–2011 mortgage lending continues to be in disarray and employment, while not double–digit, is above 8%. Oh, and there's this little thing called a presidential election occurring in November of 2012. And not one of these facts will influence the sustainability of the American economy in 2012.

My thoughts on the economy:

- The American economy will continue to expand with Gross Domestic Product (GDP) near 3% through 2012.
- Unemployment will remain in the 8% range as employees re–tool their skills and baby–boomers defer retirement based on the depth of this most recent recession.
- Residential housing will continue to struggle as the home–ownership rate decreases.
- Housing prices will begin to stabilize in 2013 (or later) only because population growth will begin to out–strip supply.

In 2012 stimulus (as we know it) is behind us and residential mortgage lending will remain tight. Federal Reserve policy does not affect employment and the presidential election is towards the end of the year. Where do we find guidance, reliable guidance about the course of the American economy?

Start with Facts, Economic Facts
Is economics science or social science? Is it a predictor of future outcomes or just a crystal ball? In my view it is science with a layer of human psychology.

Whereas Google may employ the top technology brains in the world, it's the gaming industry that has high–powered psychologist on staff. Surprised? Who better to predict how to part the un–wary gambler from their money?

Back to economics. There is not a single large bank without a Chief Economist. Part of their job is to predict economic **behavior** in markets, sometime by region or country. They **influence** the decision–making of executives charged with guiding the investment criterion of the bank's capital and that of its clients. Often, a single event will require these economists to modify their **predictions** (changes in Egypt, the BP oil spill in the gulf).

Hark! If this is science, how is it that words utilized to describe it include behavior, influence and predictions? Why not use words like outcomes, correlation and results? Because the outcomes, correlations and results are all based on behavior, influence and predictions.

Who Has Real Facts? Economic Facts

So who should we listen to? Which sooth–Sayers have standing? Following are sources of economic data that avoid providing "middle–of–the–road", data goop (data goop: information with no defining use).
Each of the following has a deep and meaningful institutional knowledge base with roots in the science of economics. These sources can assist you in building your own predictions and forecast.

Bloomberg Survey of Economist. The Survey provides a collective prediction of data points of valuable and consistent insight on the direction of the overall U.S. economy. http://bloomberg.com

International Monetary Fund. This world body is not without its internal politics. But there is no doubt they provide reporting accomplished by big brains with deep knowledge and experience within their specialties. http://www.imf.org/external/index.htm

The International Monetary Fund predicts growth in the world economy will accelerate to 4.5 percent in 2012 from 4.4 percent this year. While advanced economies will expand 2.4 percent this year, developing nations will grow 6.5 percent, driven by expansions in China and India, the IMF predicts. Bloomberg Reporters: Stephen Treloar and Josiane Kremer, May 13, 2011.
Bureau of Labor Statistics. This agency is more government

issue than U.S. greenbacks. They are tattooed with <u>facts</u> about the American labor market. I believe them to be reliable reporters providing quality information about the U.S. economy. <u>http://www.bls.gov/</u>

Certainly, there are other sources with quality information. May I suggest starting here towards building your own list of quality sources of economic information.

Top Ten Multifamily Websites

There are many websites focused exclusively on multifamily real estate. The focus of this top ten list of multifamily websites is to highlight those providing solid, current, quality content.

Some of the sites are regional, some global. Some are exclusively multifamily while others only have multifamily as part of the greater real estate asset class. All can add to our knowledge base about the multifamily business.

PREA (Pension Real Estate Association) is the best example. They allow us mere mortals access to <u>current</u> research papers written by Masters and PhD candidates supported by their organization and members. We thank them for this glimpse into the future of real estate.

10. **Multifamily Insight**. A website for owners, operators and investors in multifamily real estate. Providing content specific to the multifamily marketplace and free white papers on subjects specific to the industry. Go to Free White Papers to see the list of available reports. There are additional free reports under the Software tab.

9. **USC Lusk Center for Real Estate**. High quality data with statistical information related to southern California. Covers all real estate asset classes including multifamily.

8. **Real Estate Center at Texas A&M University**. All things "Texas" real estate including multifamily. Very detailed for the state but also has databases covering the nation.

7. **PowerHour Webcast**. Providing free hour–long web cast on topics specific to the multifamily industry.

6. **Multifamily Biz**. A multifamily portal providing blogs, and a real–time industry specific news feeds including Information on multifamily conferences nationwide, products and trends.

5. **MIT Center for Real Estate.** Provides information covering national and global trends in real estate including multifamily. Touching on subjects from global capital flows to sustainability.

4. **IREM**. Institute of Real Estate Management. The property management mega–site offers more than just information on professional designations. IREM is an affiliate of the National Association of Realtors.

3. **Units Magazine**. A publication featuring news and news makers in the multifamily housing industry. Features include interviews of members and topical articles about residential property management and ownership.

2. **Multifamily Executive**.   Provides apartment executives with apartment and condo industry news, multifamily design ideas and apartment technology information.

1. **Pension Real Estate Association**.   The Pension Real Estate Association (PREA) is a non–profit trade association for the global institutional real estate investment industry. To access current research reports, select the Research and Market Information tab. Then select Real Estate Research Institute.

Saving the Economy

Housing alone cannot save the American economy. Whereas it is an integral part of the consumer persona, relying on home ownership as a baseline cornerstone to modern economics is a misnomer.

Pre–recession, the home ownership rate peaked at just over 70%. For decades the economy has relied on housing to pull it forward out of recessionary cycles, as a job creator and bellwether of better times. As Reinhart and Rogoff state so aptly in their book– This Time is Different (This Time Is Different: Eight Centuries of Financial Folly). While housing is a major component of the economy, housing cannot save the American Economy.

The wealthiest farmer in Tyson's Corner Virginia built his fortune buying land by the acre and selling it by the square foot. Land ownership is not a new concept; land ownership by the square foot is, however.

Economist suggest that nearly seventy percent of the economy is driven by consumers; consumers that buy stuff. One of the things consumers buy is housing. Home owners buy even more stuff to enhance the value of their investment.

Most of us can remember being in our grandparents home. Most of our grandparents owned homes. But thinking back two generations prior to your grandparents, aside from family farms, do you know if your family owned a home? In the 1800's most of America was open space with "homesteads" in the west and large land owners otherwise.

On large working farms and ranches housing was part of payment for work. In cities, there was a great deal of "company housing". Rental housing ownership was concentrated also. Unlike voting, home ownership was, as it is today, a privilege– not a right.

As the home ownership rate drops, there are fewer "homeowners" in need of paint, shrubs, shiny appliances and new windows.

Thus, this impacts the economy because renters and multifamily property owners are far less likely to spend on such things as do homeowners.

The United States has strong and longstanding institutions in education, science, medicine and government. The United States has a well established force of law, property rights and a compelling social safety net un–matched by any country of similar size.

This is a great country. To retain our greatness requires continued evolution in and expansion of our intellectual capacity to identify, build and implement avenues to extend plausible economic growth. This is a collective effort requiring participation from all segments of the economy– not just housing.

Energy, Food and Multifamily Rents

Energy, food and multifamily rents are all higher now than in 2001. But how much higher? Whereas food tends to fluctuate, fuel and rents, people believe, only go up. Is this true? Let's look at some recent trends.

All three categories overlap in some manner. A big part of the costs of food is dependent on transportation costs (Energy). For multifamily, rents will sometimes depend on distances and commute times to job centers. So, we start with energy.

Energy

Energy. The average price of a gallon of gasoline in May 2001 was $1.66. In May of 2011 it was $3.78 http://eia.gov/oli–gas. This represents an average annual increase of 8.26% each year (every year for ten years). In the last twenty years the price of a barrel of oil has fluctuated from as low as $10 to as high as $140. Today it's $97 per barrel, continuing outside of the historic $35–$75 per barrel range.

Food

Food. According to http://guardian.co.uk, the Food Price Index in May of 2001 was 94. In May of 2011 it was 232.2. This represents an annual increase of 9.08% each year (every year for ten years). The costs of food production is also heavily tied to the price of energy. All along the food chain energy is expended for production– from planting through harvesting and delivery to the end users.

Rents

Rents. According to the U.S. Department of Commerce, rents have increased only one percentage point each year for the last ten years. The average cost of a two–bedroom apartment in Denver in May of 2001 was $832. In May 2011 it was $1,007 (http://statjump.com and http://hud.gov). This represents an annual increase of 1.91% each year.

Interesting. While Energy and Food have approached double digit annual growth for a decade, rents (while having fluctuated) increased only 2%. Granted, this is a micro example having depicted only a single city. Like politics, all rents are local. San Francisco and Boston are higher, Detroit and Dayton, lower.

So the answer is yes; all categories have increased in absolute dollars over the past ten years. However, rents gained the least amount in the examples presented here.

This will not hold. Rents are poised to increase with the convergence of low construction starts and population gains. Rents may not gain at the same pace as energy and food, however, but I predict a repeat of this exercise ten years from now will reflect rental increases significantly higher than those represented in the last decade. Starting in 2011.

Housing and Being Brown in America

What does being brown in America have to do with housing? Frankly, not as much as it used to, thankfully. At least from an access perspective.

As background, in the last two generations we have enacted laws that attempt to assure all people are treated equally with respect to access to housing. These laws became a necessity because of people being denied housing simply based on the color of their skin– not because of their credit rating or job status. These were never checked as the barriers were so high (and arbitrary) that obtaining an application for rent was out was of the question.

Color has become less important over time for a number of reasons. One example is the use of people of color in network advertising as a not–so–subtle medium that permeates participants psyche over time. Over years, the melting pot of America has become accustom to brown. The work product and face of Serena Williams and Maya Angelou are known world–wide.

Seldom does a person purchase a product after a single exposure to an ad– that's why repetition is key to brand advertising. Thus, over time, through various media brown has become more accepted. To wit:

Jackie Robinson– 1950's. Martin Luther King– 1960's. Jimmie Hendrix– 1970's. Michael Jordon– 1980's. Bill Cosby – 1990's. Tiger Woods and Denzel Washington– 2000's. President Barack Obama – today. There are many more, of course. This is just a sample from various professions over decades. Trailblazers all over a fifty year time table. But also, just people that excelled at their craft.

Now– to the core of the matter
This is not a post about social justice. The core of the matter presented here is the correlation between net worth and homeownership. According to a report by Sabrina Tavernise in the New York Times on July 26, 2011:

"the median net worth of Whites is now 20 times that of Black households and 18 times that of Hispanic households.

According to the Pew Research Center, in the recent recession, Whites net worth decreased 16% while the net worth of Hispanics decreased 66% and 53% for Blacks. Why? Why such a disparity? In my view this difference rest squarely on the percentage of home ownership by each race.

From the same article by Sabrina Tavernise, here is the average net worth of families by race in 2009 from the Pew Research Center:

- Hispanics: $6,235
- Blacks: $5,677
- Whites: $113,149
- Asians: $78,066

This is breathtaking. (Question: how does society have a sincere discussion on the possibility of parity? I present no remedies here, nor place responsibility for change on any one group. This blog is about housing.)

From a paper entitled <u>Race, Homeownership and Wealth</u> by Thomas M. Shapiro (Washington University– St. Louis) Mr. Shapiro states the following:

Homeownership and housing appreciation is the foundation of institutional accumulation. Indeed, for most Americans, home equity represents the largest reservoir of wealth...

Homeownership is the largest component of the wealth portfolios of both white and black families...

Conclusion: a lower homeownership rate equals lower net worth. Continuing today, there is a full twenty percentage point differential between the homeownership rate between Whites and Blacks. This is reflected in net worth.

We look forward to the day when color is a non–issue in the homeownership decision–making process. We are not there yet– regarding neighborhood selection, red–lining and financing. This will occur when educational attainment reaches parity. Education is the third leg of the chair; net worth is to homeownership as educational attainment is to opportunity. Education completes the circle.

Index

A

B

C

D

E

F

M

N

O

P

R

39365620R00124

Made in the USA
Middletown, DE
12 January 2017